SMITHSONIAN
Children's Illustrated
Animal
ATLAS

DK | Penguin Random House

Author Jamie Ambrose
Editor Olivia Stanford
Project editor Allison Singer
Project art editor Hoa Luc
Designer Rhea Gaughan
US Senior editor Shannon Beatty
US Editor Jane Perlmutter

Map illustrator Jeongeun Park
Cartography Ed Merritt, Simon Mumford
Illustrators Maltings Partnership, Molly Lattin, Bettina Myklebust Stovne, Oliver Magee
Additional design Lucy Sims, Yamini Panwar
Assistant editor Prerna Grewal
Jacket coordinator Francesca Young
Jacket designer Hoa Luc
Managing editor Laura Gilbert
Managing art editor Diane Peyton Jones
Senior Pre-producer Nikoleta Parasaki
Producer Niamh Tierney
Art director Martin Wilson
Publisher Sarah Larter
Publishing director Sophie Mitchell

First American Edition, 2017
Published in the United States by DK Publishing
1745 Broadway, 20th Floor, New York, NY 10019

Copyright © 2017 Dorling Kindersley Limited.
DK, a Division of Penguin Random House LLC
23 24 25 10 9 8 7 6
020–298819–Aug/2017

A catalog record for this book
is available from the Library of Congress.
ISBN: 978-1-4654-6203-9

DK books are available at special discounts when purchased in bulk for sales promotions, premiums, fund-raising, or educational use. For details, contact: DK Publishing Special Markets, 1745 Broadway, 20th Floor, New York, NY 10019
SpecialSales@dk.com

Printed and bound in the UAE

www.dk.com

MIX
Paper | Supporting responsible forestry
FSC™ C018179

This book was made with Forest Stewardship Council™ certified paper—one small step in DK's commitment to a sustainable future. For more information go to www.dk.com/our-green-pledge

Contents

Smithsonian

This trademark is owned by the Smithsonian Institution and
is registered in the U.S Patent and Trademark Office.

Consultant Dr. Don E. Wilson, Curator Emeritus, Department of Vertebrate Zoology,
National Museum of Natural History, Smithsonian

Smithsonian Enterprises
Product Development Manager Kealy Gordon
Licensing Manager Ellen Nanney
Vice President, Consumer and Education Products Brigid Ferraro
Senior Vice President, Consumer and Education Products Carol LeBlanc
President Christopher A. Liedel

Established in 1846, the Smithsonian Institution—the world's largest museum and
research complex—includes 19 museums and galleries and the National Zoological Park.
The total number of objects, works of art, and specimens in the Smithsonian's collection is
estimated at 154 million. The Smithsonian is a renowned research center, dedicated to
public education, national service, and scholarship in the arts, sciences, and history.

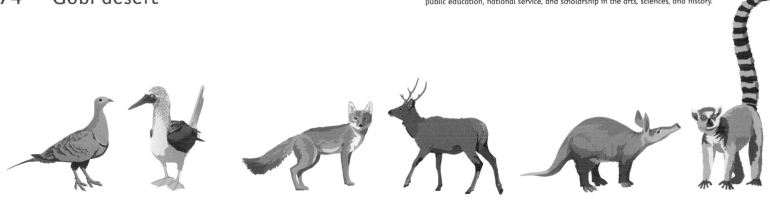

How to use this book

An atlas usually shows maps of different countries, but animals often live across borders. The maps in this book show many of the world's different habitats, which is the environment where an animal lives, such as a desert. Some islands are also shown, since they have animals that are found nowhere else.

Compass
The compass always points north (N) in line with the map. It also shows the direction of south (S), east (E), and west (W).

Animal pictures
Pictures with descriptions pick out particular animals that live in an area.

Independent states
Small independent states, such as Monaco, are shown with a red border and a solid red dot, and the name is in capital letters.

Rivers
Each country's largest rivers are shown as continuous blue lines.

Mediterranean scrubland

The coastal areas around the Mediterranean Sea contain rocky hills and flat, shrub-filled plains. This rare habitat is found in only a few places on Earth. Plants here can survive wildfires, and animals have to deal with hot, dry weather.

Mediterranean chameleon
This is one of only two chameleon species found in Europe. Its tongue is sticky to catch passing insects. It is also twice the length of its body!

Hummingbird hawk moth
This insect beats its wings so fast that they make a humming sound—just like the birds it's named after. It feeds on nectar made by flowers like buddleia and honeysuckle.

The hawk moth will return to a nectar-rich flower day after day.

Iberian lynx
Just 404 adult Iberian lynxes are left in the wild, so this is the most endangered cat on Earth—but the good news is this figure is nearly twice the number of wild lynxes alive a few years ago!

The Iberian lynx mostly hunts just one animal—the European rabbit.

This wolf is thinner and smaller than other European wolves. It hunts rabbits, deer, wild boar, birds, and fish.

FRANCE

Garonne

Rhône

Ebro

Iberian wolf

PORTUGAL

Madrid

Lisbon

Tagus

This monkey is found in Africa and on the island of Gibraltar, near Spain. It is the only wild monkey in Europe.

Iberian pig
This pig is a farmed animal, but lives in open country, looking for mushrooms, roots, and acorns from cork oaks.

Barbary macaque

SPAIN

ANDORRA

PYRENEES

Iberian ibex

A type of wild goat, male Iberian ibexes have horns that grow up to 29½ in (75 cm) long!

Mediterranean tree frog
This frog is usually bright green or blue. It has suckers on its fingers and toes that let it climb with ease.

Mediterranean banded centipede
This centipede paralyzes its prey with a venomous bite and will give a human a painful nip too—so stay well away!

Jeweled lizard

The sapphire-like blue spots on its body give this lizard its name. It is the largest lizard in Europe at about 23½ in (60 cm) long.

Majorca

MONACO

SAN MARINO

ITALY

Rome

VATICAN CITY

The cuckoo lays its eggs in other birds' nests. When the cuckoo chick hatches, it pushes all the other eggs out—so the parent birds feed it instead!

Common cuckoo

Corsica

Sardinia

The golden jackal is found in many places, including southeastern Europe, northern Africa, and southern Asia.

Golden jackal

Zagreb

CROATIA

BOSNIA & HERZEGOVINA

Sarajevo

Belgrade

ROMANIA

SERBIA

MONTENEGRO

Podgorica

Pristina

KOSOVO

Skopje

BULGARIA

MACEDONIA

Tirana

ALBANIA

ADRIATIC SEA

The cork oak is one of few trees that can grow new bark. The cork bark is harvested once every nine years to make bottle stoppers and other items.

Cork oak

The magpie is so smart that it can make and use tools. It eats insects and seeds, and will even steal other birds' eggs.

Eurasian magpie

Dalmatian pelican

In addition to making other sounds, this pelican barks and hisses! When fishing, it fills up its beak with food to eat later.

GREECE

Marginated tortoise

This plant-eating tortoise lives mostly in Greece, in thorny, rocky, scrubby areas.

Athens

MEDITERRANEAN SEA

Sicily

MEDITERRANEAN SEA

MALTA

Crete

SCALE
0 — 200 miles
0 — 200 kilometers

HABITAT KEY
Scrublands | Coniferous forests
Wetlands | Deciduous forests
Mountains

European rabbit
The European rabbit is the ancestor of all pet rabbits in the world. Unlike its enemy, the Iberian lynx, the rabbit has been seen in yards and parks, and even in busy cities.

Location
This region includes the southern parts of Europe around the Mediterranean Sea, as well as islands like Crete that share a similar habitat.

Mediterranean house gecko
This little gecko is about 4 in (10 cm) long and weighs about as much as a sugar cube. It is also called a "moon lizard" because it mostly comes out at night. It eats small cockroaches and moths.

Capital
A country's capital city is marked with a red outline. Some countries have more than one capital city.

Scale
The scale shows the size of the areas and the distances between different points on the map.

Location
The location box shows you where each area is found in relation to the land around it.

Habitat key
Every map has a key that lists the types of habitats found in that area.

Bordering continents
Around the edges of some maps you can see parts of bordering continents in a cream color.

North America

This continent stretches from the icy Arctic down to the tropical Caribbean. It is a vast range of habitats, from snow-covered mountains to lush rain forests, and is home to millions of different animals—some large, some small, and all amazing.

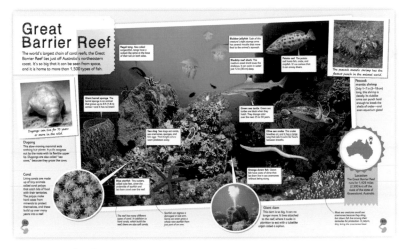

Great Barrier Reef

The world's largest chain of coral reefs, the Great Barrier Reef lies just off Australia's northeastern coast. It's so big that it can be seen from space, and it is home to more than 1,500 types of fish.

Continent maps

The continent maps are colored to show the biomes found on each continent. A biome is a large area of one type of habitat, and the animals and plants in it. Photographs show some of the places in these biomes.

Feature habitats

The feature spreads show a specific place and some of the animals that live there. In reality, not all the animals would be found together at the same time, since they are awake at different times of day, and would often avoid each other to prevent being eaten!

Habitats

These symbols show the different types of habitat on each map.

 Mountains
High, rugged mountainous areas are often covered with snow.

 Coniferous forests
Trees in coniferous forests usually have needlelike leaves that are kept all year round.

 Wetlands
Wetlands are marshy, swampy areas, such as the Pantanal in Brazil.

 Hot desert
Hot deserts, such as the Sahara, are dry, sandy areas. Few plants grow here.

 Oceans and seas
Huge stretches of water are found around the Earth's seven continents.

 Mangroves
Mangrove trees grow on coasts in salty water. Their long roots stick out of the water.

 Temperate grasslands
Flat, grassy plains with few trees found in seasonal areas are temperate grasslands, such as prairie, steppe, and pampas.

 Cold desert
Cold deserts, such as the Gobi, are cold, dry stretches of land.

 Tropical forests
Rain forests, such as the Amazon, get a lot of rain and heat so the trees grow very tall.

 Tropical coral reefs
Tropical coral reefs grow in shallow waters. They are built by coral animals.

Tropical grasslands
Flat, grassy plains with few trees found in hot areas are tropical grasslands, such as savanna and cerrado.

 Snow and ice
Frozen areas are found high up in the mountains and at the North and South Poles.

 Deciduous forests
Most trees in deciduous forests have broad leaves that are lost in the fall, or during the dry season.

 Scrublands
Low-lying plants and grasses grow in scrubland areas with small trees, such as in southern Spain.

Borders

Borders show how the Earth's land is divided into countries.

 Country borders
The borders between countries are shown with a broken white line.

 Disputed borders
Some countries disagree about where the border between them should be. These borders are shown with a white dotted line.

 Continent borders
A broken orange line shows where the border is between two continents.

5

ARCTIC OCEAN

NORTH AMERICA

Arctic Circle
The Arctic Circle shows where the temperate zone ends and the cold northern polar region begins.

ATLANTIC OCEAN

EUROPE

Tropic of Cancer
This line marks the northern limit of the tropics. Above this is the Northern Hemisphere's temperate zone.

PACIFIC OCEAN

AFRICA

Equator
This is an imaginary line that goes around the middle of the Earth, dividing it into two halves, called the Northern and Southern Hemispheres.

SOUTH AMERICA

The world

The types of habitats found on each of the Earth's seven continents depend on the usual weather, or climate, of an area. Five invisible lines divide the world into three climatic zones: the tropical zone is hot, the temperate zones are seasonal, and the polar zones are cold.

Tropic of Capricorn
This line marks the southern limit of the tropics. Below this is the Southern Hemisphere's temperate zone.

ATLANTIC OCEAN

SOUTHERN OCEAN

Antarctic Circle
The Antarctic Circle shows where the temperate zone ends and the cold southern polar region begins.

ARCTIC OCEAN

EUROPE

ASIA

Polar zone
Inside the polar circles,
around the North and
South Poles, it is dry
and very cold.

Temperate zone
Both temperate zones
have warm summers and
cold winters. Forests in the
temperate zone often lose
their leaves in the fall or
during the dry season.

PACIFIC
OCEAN

Tropical zone
The area between
the tropics, around the
equator, is very hot.
Most rain forests are
found in this zone.

INDIAN
OCEAN

AUSTRALASIA

Temperate zone

SOUTHERN OCEAN

ANTARCTICA

Polar zone

North America

This continent stretches from the icy Arctic down to the tropical Caribbean. It has a vast range of habitats, from snow-covered mountains to lush rain forests, and is home to millions of different animals—some large, some small, and all amazing.

California coast redwoods

These redwood trees can grow more than 350 ft (107 m) high and live up to 2,000 years. Bears, owls, and other woodland creatures—including a banana slug—call them home.

Western mountains

The rocky peaks and thick coniferous forests in the mountains of western North America are filled with wildlife. Wolves, deer, and grizzly bears roam freely here, while in the fjords (narrow inlets), bald eagles hunt for salmon.

HAWAII
(UNITED STATES)

Great Plains

With thousands of miles of grassland, the dry Great Plains can appear empty. Look closer, though, and you'll see big bison, as well as prairie dogs hiding in their secret world of underground burrows.

Map labels:

ARCTIC OCEAN

BERING SEA

BEAUFORT SEA

ALASKA
(UNITED STATES)

Yukon Territory

Northwest Territories

British Columbia

Alberta

PACIFIC OCEAN

Washington

Montana

Oregon

Idaho

UNITED STATES

Nevada

Utah

California

Arizona

HABITAT KEY

- Tropical forests
- Deciduous forests
- Coniferous forests
- Tropical grasslands
- Scrublands
- Temperate grasslands
- Desert
- Wetlands
- Tundra
- Ice
- Mangroves

GREENLAND
(DENMARK)

Nunavut

Newfoundland & Labrador

CANADA

Saskatchewan

Manitoba

Ontario

Québec

Prince
Edward
Island

ST. PIERRE
& MIQUELON
(FRANCE)

New
Brunswick

Nova Scotia

Maine

Barrier islands
These long, thin stretches of sand protect the
mainland from powerful storms. The barrier
islands off the Virginia and Maryland coasts
are home to the wild Chincoteague Ponies
of Chincoteague and Assateague islands.

Central American rain forest
Tropical rain forests are warm and
green all year, and they are home to
more than half the world's
plant and animal species.
These colorful scarlet
macaws from Costa
Rica perch high in
rain-forest trees.

North
Dakota

Minnesota

Wisconsin

Michigan

New York

Vermont

New Hampshire

Massachusetts

Rhode Island

Connecticut

South
Dakota

Wyoming

Nebraska

Iowa

Illinois

Indiana

Ohio

Pennsylvania

New Jersey

Delaware

Maryland

West
Virginia

Virginia

Colorado

Kansas

Missouri

Kentucky

North Carolina

BERMUDA
(UNITED KINGDOM)

New Mexico

Oklahoma

Arkansas

Tennessee

South Carolina

OF AMERICA (USA)

Texas

Mississippi

Alabama

Georgia

Louisiana

Florida

ATLANTIC OCEAN

GULF OF MEXICO

BAHAMAS

BRITISH
VIRGIN ISLANDS
(UNITED KINGDOM)

ANGUILLA (UNITED KINGDOM)

PUERTO RICO
(UNITED STATES)

ST. KITTS & NEVIS

ANTIGUA & BARBUDA

MONTSERRAT (UNITED KINGDOM)

CUBA

DOMINICA

MEXICO

HAITI

DOMINICAN
REPUBLIC

US VIRGIN
ISLANDS
(UNITED STATES)

MARTINIQUE (FRANCE)

BARBADOS

JAMAICA

CARIBBEAN SEA

ST. LUCIA
GRENADA

ST. VINCENT & THE GRENADINES

CURACAO
(NETHERLANDS)

TRINIDAD & TOBAGO

BELIZE

ARUBA
(NETHERLANDS)

GUATEMALA

HONDURAS

EL SALVADOR

NICARAGUA

COSTA RICA

PANAMA

SCALE

0   500 miles   1000 miles

0   1000 kilometers

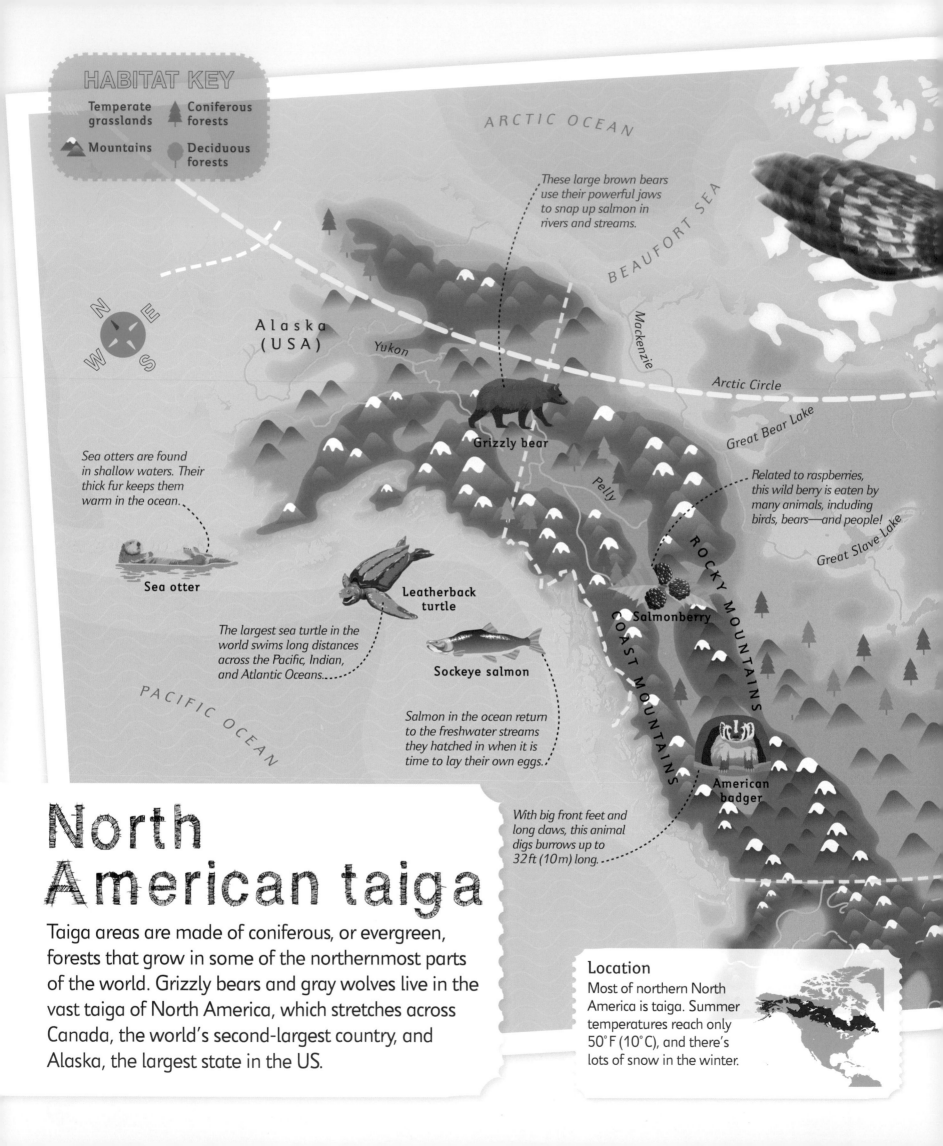

Temperate grasslands

Coniferous forests

Mountains

Deciduous forests

ARCTIC OCEAN

BEAUFORT SEA

These large brown bears use their powerful jaws to snap up salmon in rivers and streams.

Alaska (USA)

Yukon

Mackenzie

Arctic Circle

Great Bear Lake

Grizzly bear

Pelly

Related to raspberries, this wild berry is eaten by many animals, including birds, bears—and people!

Great Slave Lake

Sea otters are found in shallow waters. Their thick fur keeps them warm in the ocean.

Sea otter

ROCKY MOUNTAINS

COAST MOUNTAINS

Salmonberry

Leatherback turtle

The largest sea turtle in the world swims long distances across the Pacific, Indian, and Atlantic Oceans.

Sockeye salmon

PACIFIC OCEAN

Salmon in the ocean return to the freshwater streams they hatched in when it is time to lay their own eggs.

American badger

With big front feet and long claws, this animal digs burrows up to 32 ft (10 m) long.

North American taiga

Taiga areas are made of coniferous, or evergreen, forests that grow in some of the northernmost parts of the world. Grizzly bears and gray wolves live in the vast taiga of North America, which stretches across Canada, the world's second-largest country, and Alaska, the largest state in the US.

Location
Most of northern North America is taiga. Summer temperatures reach only 50°F (10°C), and there's lots of snow in the winter.

Great gray owl
North America's tallest owl has a wingspan of up to 5 ft (1.5 m). It listens for rodents moving under the snow, then snatches them up.

Snow geese
Flocks of snow geese turn fields white when they land. These noisy birds live in cold areas, but fly south in large groups during the winter.

Snow geese fly south for the winter.

HUDSON BAY

This flat-tailed mammal fells trees with its teeth. It uses the logs to build dams across rivers, and lodges to live in.

The loon's legs are made for swimming, not walking— so when it wants to fly, it can only take off from water.

A moose can weigh as much as a car! It can also trot at a steady pace of 20 mph (32 kph).

Pacific loon

North American beaver

CANADA

These geese are found all over the world. They have a loud honk and fly in a V-shaped formation.

Moose

GULF OF ST LAWRENCE

ATLANTIC OCEAN

Lake Winnipeg

Canada goose

Both male and female fireflies flash yellow, green, or orange light using special organs in their tails.

Monarch butterfly

Each winter, millions of monarchs migrate from northern North America to Mexico.

Ottawa

Lake Superior   **Firefly**

Lake Huron

Lake Ontario

Lake Erie

Lake Michigan

USA

Gray wolf
The gray wolf is the largest wild member of the dog family. It can have black, white, tan, brown, or gray fur. It hunts in packs and eats animals from tiny mice to huge moose.

11

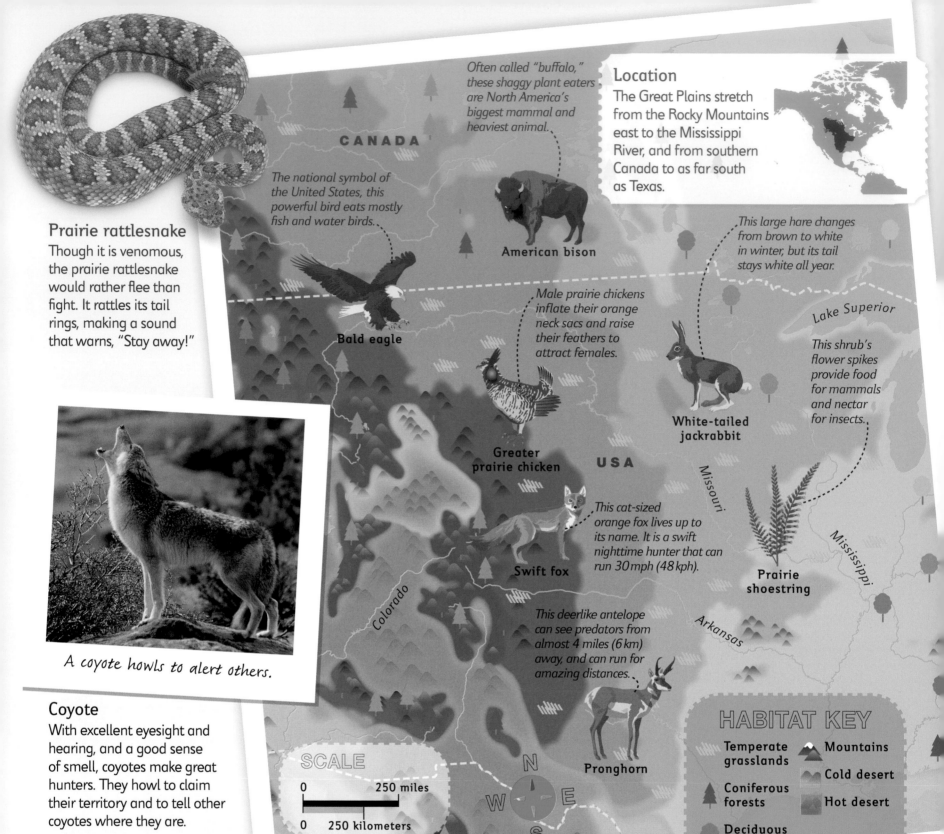

Prairie rattlesnake
Though it is venomous, the prairie rattlesnake would rather flee than fight. It rattles its tail rings, making a sound that warns, "Stay away!"

Often called "buffalo," these shaggy plant eaters are North America's biggest mammal and heaviest animal.

CANADA

Location
The Great Plains stretch from the Rocky Mountains east to the Mississippi River, and from southern Canada to as far south as Texas.

The national symbol of the United States, this powerful bird eats mostly fish and water birds.

American bison

This large hare changes from brown to white in winter, but its tail stays white all year.

Bald eagle

Male prairie chickens inflate their orange neck sacs and raise their feathers to attract females.

Lake Superior

This shrub's flower spikes provide food for mammals and nectar for insects.

White-tailed jackrabbit

Greater prairie chicken

USA

Missouri

This cat-sized orange fox lives up to its name. It is a swift nighttime hunter that can run 30 mph (48 kph).

Mississippi

Swift fox

Prairie shoestring

Colorado

This deerlike antelope can see predators from almost 4 miles (6 km) away, and can run for amazing distances.

Arkansas

A coyote howls to alert others.

Coyote
With excellent eyesight and hearing, and a good sense of smell, coyotes make great hunters. They howl to claim their territory and to tell other coyotes where they are.

SCALE
0 ———— 250 miles
0 ———— 250 kilometers

N W E S

Pronghorn

HABITAT KEY
Temperate grasslands
Mountains
Coniferous forests
Cold desert
Hot desert
Deciduous forests

Great Plains

The Great Plains are in the center of North America. Made of high prairie about 3,000 miles (4,800 km) long, they were once home to thousands of bison and antelope. Today farmland has taken over much of the area, and it's mostly cattle herds who wander the plains, but wildlife has found ways to survive.

Black-tailed prairie dog
These grass-eating rodents live in underground prairie-dog towns. They greet family with a kiss, and have different warning calls for different predators.

Gray fox

As big as a medium-sized dog, gray foxes live in broad-leaved forests. They make their dens in hollow trees, and both parents care for the cubs.

Eastern forests

Deciduous and coniferous forests cover eastern North America. There are mountains and river valleys here, too. Animals have to be smart to survive in areas densely populated with humans.

CANADA

If threatened, the skunk sprays a horrible-smelling musk from glands under its tail.

Lake Superior

Sugar maples provide sap for maple syrup. Their leaves turn orange-gold and red in the fall.

Raccoons are highly intelligent. They can live in towns or the country and will eat almost anything!

Lake Michigan

USA

Only male deer grow antlers. White-tails often escape predators by swimming across lakes or rivers.

Ohio

Striped skunk

Sugar maple

SCALE

0   250 miles

0   250 kilometers

This bright-red bird can sing more than 24 songs. When courting, males offer females the best seeds.

Northern raccoon

Northern cardinal

Washington, D.C.

White-tailed deer

Mississippi

This is North America's only marsupial. It can outsmart danger by playing dead for up to four hours.

Great horned owl

Virginia opossum

ATLANTIC OCEAN

This large owl's feathery "horns" look like ears, but its real ears are much farther down on its skull.

Despite their name, gray squirrels can also have white or reddish fur.

HABITAT KEY

⩗ Temperate grasslands	▲ Coniferous forests
⩗ Tropical grasslands	● Deciduous forests
⛰ Mountains	

N
W   E
S

Gray squirrel

Double-jointed ankles help gray squirrels scamper up and down trees. Their teeth never stop growing, to make up for how they are worn down by chewing nuts and tree bark.

American black bear

Good swimmers and climbers, black bears feast on fruits, nuts, and roots, and sometimes ants and grubs. There are twice as many of them in the world as there are all other bear species combined.

Location

Most of the continent's eastern forests stretch from the Mississippi River Valley eastward, all the way to the Atlantic Ocean.

13

Western deserts

Western North America has four deserts. These dry, sandy areas are hot during the day, but at night they can get very cold. Animals here must survive these tough conditions—and with very little water.

USA

A tortoise snacks on a desert plant.

Mohave desert tortoise
This desert tortoise can live for up to 50 years. It digs a burrow to avoid the desert heat, and it spends 95 percent of its time there during the summer.

A short, or "bobbed," tail gives this wild cat its name. More than a million bobcats live in North America.

Bobcat

ROCKY MOUNTAINS

Colorado

Desert broom
The desert broom's flowers provide sweet nectar for butterflies.

This lizard lives mostly underground. It has a venomous bite and eats eggs.

Gila monster

Great Salt Lake

A turkey vulture perches on a cactus.

Turkey vulture
Turkey vultures can't kill their own prey, so they eat animals that have already died instead. Animals that behave in this way are called scavengers.

Snake

The jackrabbit can run up to 30 mph (48 kph) and jump 20 ft (6 m) into the air.

Black-tailed jackrabbit

Male bighorns fight by crashing their big heads and horns together.

Bighorn sheep

This big, hairy spider lines its desert burrow with silk to keep it from caving in.

Desert blonde tarantula

SIERRA NEVADA

14

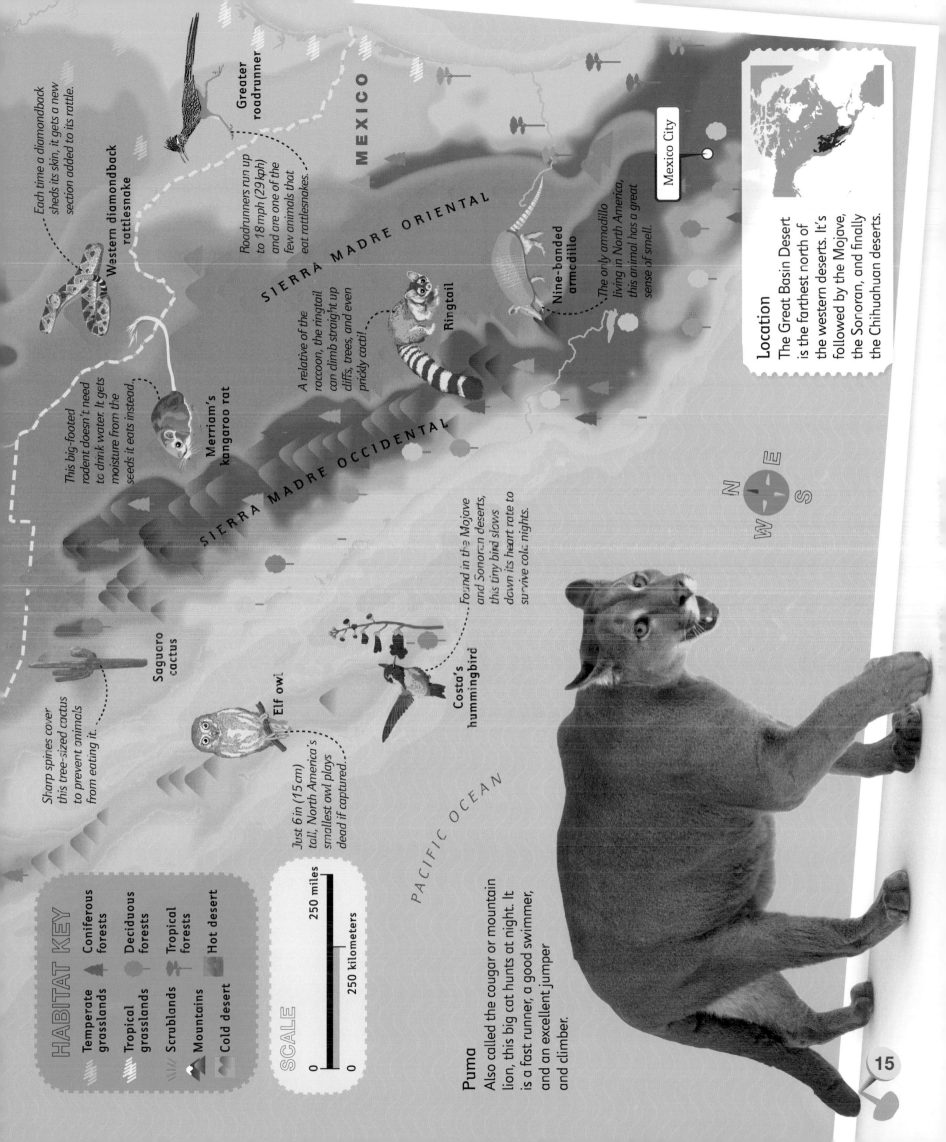

Each time a diamondback sheds its skin, it gets a new section added to its rattle.

Western diamondback rattlesnake

Greater roadrunner

Roadrunners run up to 18mph (29kph) and are one of the few animals that eat rattlesnakes.

MEXICO

SIERRA MADRE ORIENTAL

Nine-banded armadillo

The only armadillo living in North America, this animal has a great sense of smell.

Mexico City

Location
The Great Basin Desert is the farthest north of the western deserts. It's followed by the Mojave, the Sonoran, and finally the Chihuahuan deserts.

A relative of the raccoon, the ringtail can climb straight up cliffs, trees, and even prickly cacti!

Ringtail

This big-footed rodent doesn't need to drink water. It gets moisture from the seeds it eats instead.

Merriam's kangaroo rat

SIERRA MADRE OCCIDENTAL

N
W E
S

Sharp spines cover this tree-sized cactus to prevent animals from eating it.

Saguaro cactus

Elf owl

Just 6in (15cm) tall, North America's smallest owl plays dead if captured.

Found in the Mojave and Sonoran deserts, this tiny bird slows down its heart rate to survive cold nights.

Costa's hummingbird

PACIFIC OCEAN

HABITAT KEY

- Temperate grasslands
- Coniferous forests
- Deciduous forests
- Tropical grasslands
- Scrublands
- Tropical forests
- Mountains
- Hot desert
- Cold desert

SCALE

0 — 250 miles

0 — 250 kilometers

Puma

Also called the cougar or mountain lion, this big cat hunts at night. It is a fast runner, a good swimmer, and an excellent jumper and climber.

Resplendent quetzal

BELIZE

Mexican kite swallowtail butterfly

These butterflies are named for their long wing tips that look like swallows' tails.

This monkey swings through the rain forest and can hang from branches by its tail.

Location
Central America connects North and South America. Its tropical climate is ideal for plants and the animals that depend on them.

GUATEMALA

Guatemala City

This tiny bird's long, curved bill lets it sip nectar from inside rain-forest flowers.

HONDURAS

HABITAT KEY
- Mangroves
- Mountains
- Coniferous forests
- Tropical forests
- Deciduous forests

Geoffroy's spider monkey

EL SALVADOR

Tegucigalpa

A male quetzal's twin tail feathers are more than twice as long as its body.

San Salvador

Bronzy hermit hummingbird

NICARAGUA

SCALE
0   100 miles
0   100 kilometers

Managua

Tayra

The tayra hunts small monkeys, rodents, and birds, but it also eats fruit and honey.

CARIBBEAN SEA

PACIFIC OCEAN

COSTA RICA

Sticky finger pads help this little frog cling to twigs and branches.

San José

Red-eyed tree frog

It may look more like a pig, but the tapir is related to horses.

N W E S

PANAMA

Baird's tapir

Panama City

Hoffmann's two-toed sloth
Two long claws on its front legs let this slow-moving sloth get around the rain forest. It spends almost its entire life upside down!

Central America

Seven countries make up the narrow strip of land that is Central America. More than 1,500 different species of birds live here, and many more animals find food and shelter in its warm rain forests.

Ocelot
This fast cat's super sight and hearing help it hunt rabbits and other small animals at night. During the day it rests in the trees, where its markings blend in among the leaves.

USA

Havana

Nassau

BAHAMAS

CUBA

Only wild pigs live on the tiny island of Big Major Cay. They swim out to greet visitors!

Feral pig

ATLANTIC OCEAN

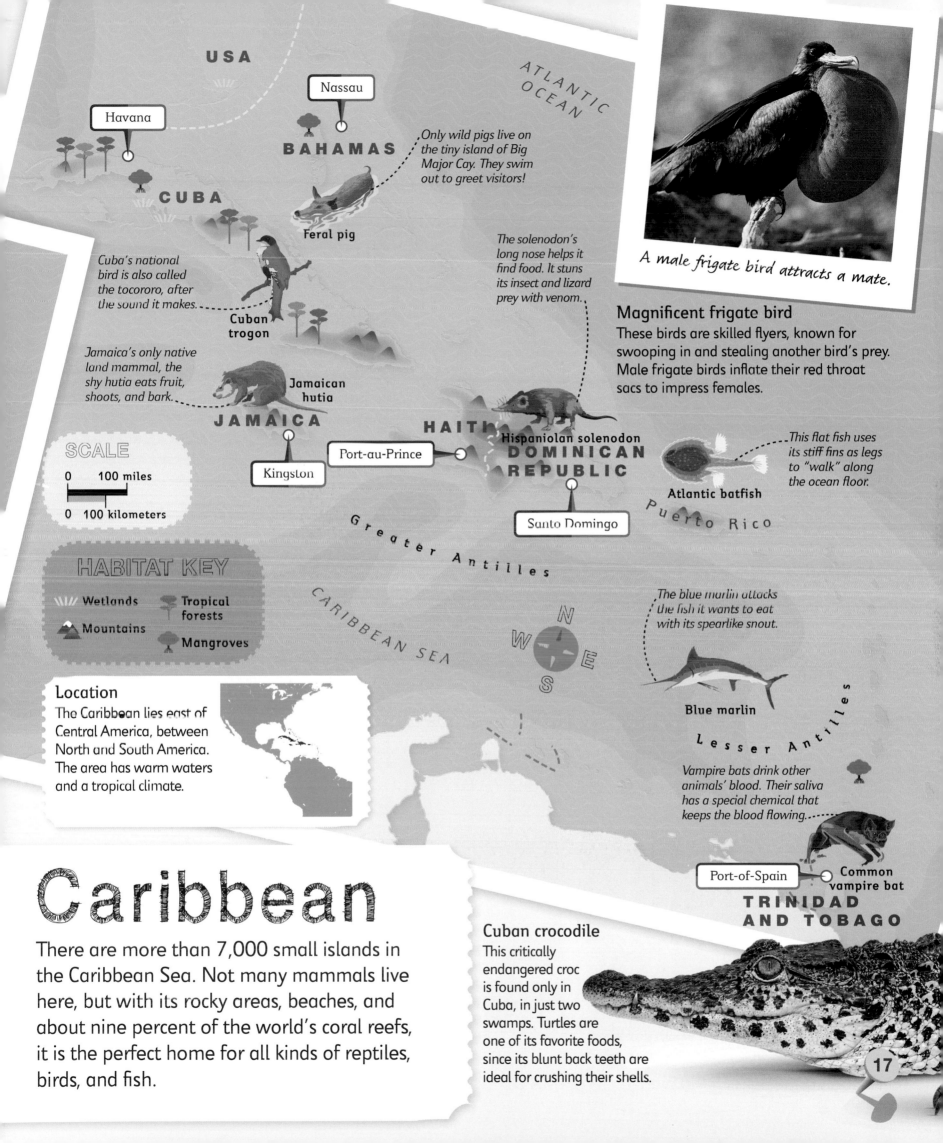

A male frigate bird attracts a mate.

Cuba's national bird is also called the tocororo, after the sound it makes.

Cuban trogon

The solenodon's long nose helps it find food. It stuns its insect and lizard prey with venom.

Magnificent frigate bird
These birds are skilled flyers, known for swooping in and stealing another bird's prey. Male frigate birds inflate their red throat sacs to impress females.

Jamaica's only native land mammal, the shy hutia eats fruit, shoots, and bark.

Jamaican hutia

JAMAICA

HAITI

Hispaniolan solenodon

DOMINICAN REPUBLIC

This flat fish uses its stiff fins as legs to "walk" along the ocean floor.

Port-au-Prince

Kingston

Santo Domingo

Atlantic batfish

Puerto Rico

SCALE
0   100 miles

0   100 kilometers

Greater Antilles

HABITAT KEY

〰️ Wetlands   🌴 Tropical forests

⛰️ Mountains

🌳 Mangroves

CARIBBEAN SEA

The blue marlin attacks the fish it wants to eat with its spearlike snout.

N
W   E
S

Blue marlin

Lesser Antilles

Location
The Caribbean lies east of Central America, between North and South America. The area has warm waters and a tropical climate.

Vampire bats drink other animals' blood. Their saliva has a special chemical that keeps the blood flowing.

Port-of-Spain

Common vampire bat

TRINIDAD AND TOBAGO

Caribbean

There are more than 7,000 small islands in the Caribbean Sea. Not many mammals live here, but with its rocky areas, beaches, and about nine percent of the world's coral reefs, it is the perfect home for all kinds of reptiles, birds, and fish.

Cuban crocodile
This critically endangered croc is found only in Cuba, in just two swamps. Turtles are one of its favorite foods, since its blunt back teeth are ideal for crushing their shells.

17

Florida Everglades

The Everglades, North America's largest subtropical wetland, is really a big, slow-moving river. The area is half its original size due to humans sending its water to farms and cities. However, it is still home to 350 bird species, and reptiles such as alligators and crocodiles.

Common snapping turtle

Although it has no teeth, this turtle's strong, bony beak and jaws can bite and kill birds, fish, and small mammals. It is also known to bite the heads off other turtles that come too close. No wonder most animals, including humans, know to leave it alone!

Around 300 fish species are found in the waters of the Everglades, ranging from tiny pygmy sunfish to barracudas that can grow up to 6 ft (2 m) long.

Great blue heron North America's largest heron is a slow smover, but it strikes fast to catch fish in mid-swim.

Anhinga This bird hunts underwater. It acts like a spear-fisherman, stabbing fish with its long, sharp bill.

American alligator The Everglades is the only place in the wild where alligators and crocodiles live together.

A rat snake shows off its forked tongue.

Everglades rat snake

This long snake both swims and can climb trees. Rats are on its menu, but it also eats frogs, squirrels, and birds and their eggs.

An alligator's teeth are hidden from sight when its mouth is closed— unlike a crocodile's, which are always visible.

Everglades snail kite This bird of prey eats apple snails. It uses its curved bill to pull the snails out of their shells.

An orb weaver sits in wait on its web.

Golden silk orb weaver
Female orb weavers can grow up to 3 in (8 cm) long. Their silk is gold in color, and it is stronger than the material used in bulletproof vests!

Purple gallinule This duck-sized bird has long toes that allow it to walk on lily pads without sinking.

Florida panther These panthers are critically endangered. Fewer than 100 are left in the wild, since so many have been hunted.

Location
The Everglades stretches across the southern tip of Florida. During its rainy season, this area gets twice as much rain as other places in the US.

Green tree frog
Depending on its mood, this little frog is either bright green or dull khaki in color. It inflates its vocal sac and screams if picked up—which can save its life, since the scream makes a lot of predators drop it in surprise!

19

South America

Earth's fourth-largest continent lies mostly in the southern half of the world. It has tropical rain forests, dry deserts, grassy plains, and high, snowy mountains. The many different habitats means that a variety of amazing animals can make South America their home.

N
W E
S

GALÁPAGOS
ISLANDS
(ECUADOR)

VENEZUELA

COLOMBIA

ECUADOR

PERU

BOLIVIA

CHILE

ARGENTINA

PACIFIC OCEAN

Amazon rain forest
The winding Amazon River flows through the enormous rain forest that shares its name. In addition to producing a fifth of the planet's oxygen, this rain forest is home to an astonishing variety of plants, mammals, birds, and fish.

Pantanal
The Pantanal is a wetland wonderland. With flooded grasslands and tropical forests, it is home to thousands of birds, fish, and reptiles. Mammals also live here, such as the plant-eating capybara, which hides from predators in the muddy waters.

HABITAT KEY

- Tropical forests
- Deciduous forests
- Tropical grasslands
- Scrublands
- Temperate grasslands
- Deserts
- Wetlands
- Mountains
- Mangroves

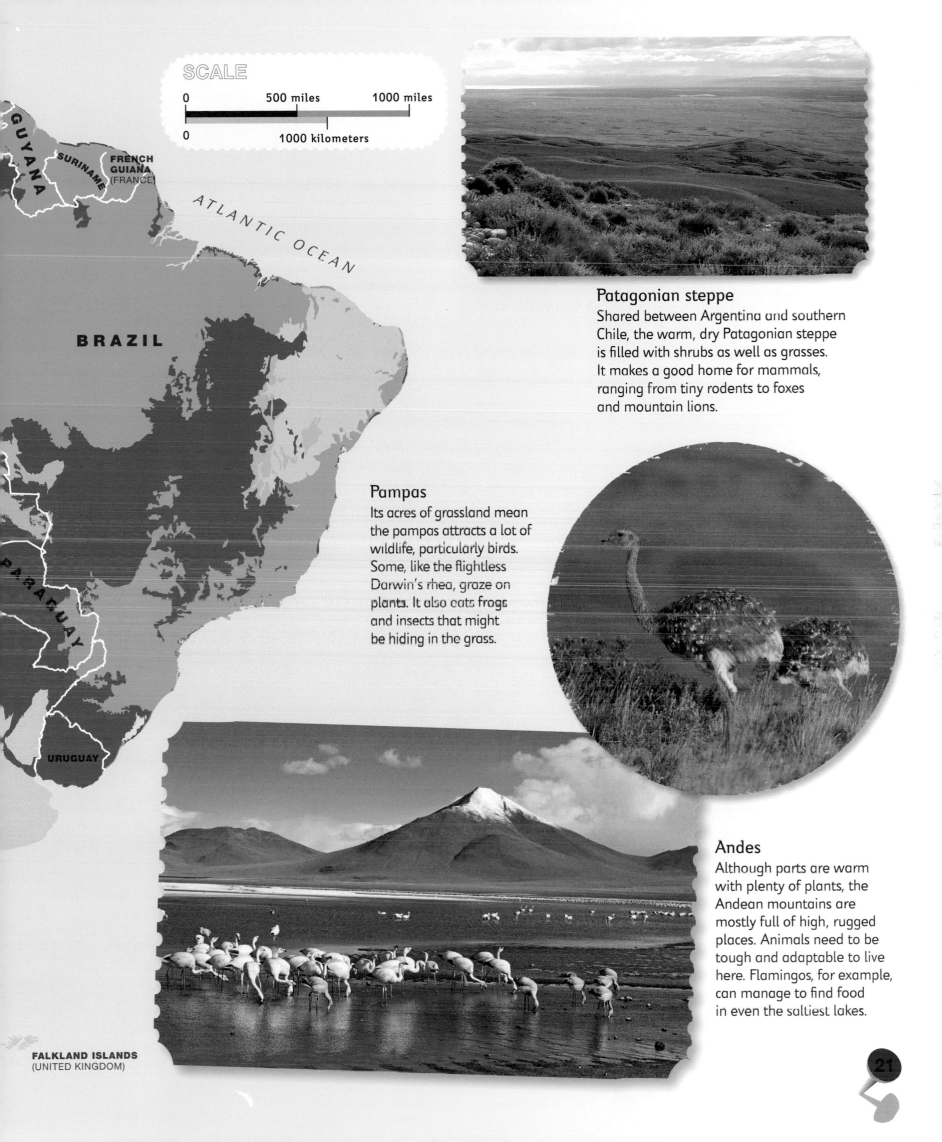

0   500 miles   1000 miles

0   1000 kilometers

GUYANA

SURINAME

FRENCH GUIANA (FRANCE)

ATLANTIC OCEAN

BRAZIL

PARAGUAY

URUGUAY

FALKLAND ISLANDS (UNITED KINGDOM)

Patagonian steppe

Shared between Argentina and southern Chile, the warm, dry Patagonian steppe is filled with shrubs as well as grasses. It makes a good home for mammals, ranging from tiny rodents to foxes and mountain lions.

Pampas

Its acres of grassland mean the pampas attracts a lot of wildlife, particularly birds. Some, like the flightless Darwin's rhea, graze on plants. It also eats frogs and insects that might be hiding in the grass.

Andes

Although parts are warm with plenty of plants, the Andean mountains are mostly full of high, rugged places. Animals need to be tough and adaptable to live here. Flamingos, for example, can manage to find food in even the saltiest lakes.

Amazon rain forest

The Amazon is the Earth's largest tropical rain forest, and it surrounds one of the world's largest rivers—the Amazon River. Lots of species live here, including more than 430 mammals, 1,300 birds, 3,000 fish, 870 reptiles and amphibians, and 2.5 million insects!

A young collared anteater rides on its mother's back.

Collared anteater

This tree-climbing anteater doesn't have any teeth. Instead it slurps up ants and termites with a tongue that can be 16 in (40 cm) long!

Yellow-banded poison dart frog

This frog's bright-yellow color tells predators to keep away. It is a serious warning, since its skin oozes toxic chemicals that can kill other animals.

22

Caracas

VENEZUELA

Orinoco

GUIANA HIGHLANDS

Bogotá

COLOMBIA

One of the largest beetles in the world, the Hercules can get up to 7 in (18 cm) long.

Hercules beetle

Quito

This tree can grow 13 ft (4 m) a year. It is pollinated by rain-forest bats.

ECUADOR

Also called botos, these rare dolphins hunt catfish in the Amazon and Orinoco Rivers.

Kapok tree

Pink river dolphin

PERU

Just 9–10 in (23–26 cm) long, this little primate eats mostly fruit, insects, and plants.

This giant blue butterfly has a wingspan of 5–8 in (13–20 cm).

ANDES

Emperor tamarin

Blue morpho

PACIFIC OCEAN

Lima

La Paz

HABITAT KEY

- Wetlands
- Tropical grasslands
- Mountains
- Tropical forests
- Deciduous forests
- Mangroves

N W E S

Sucre

Most of the Amazon is found in Brazil, but it extends into eight other countries. It is very hot and wet—it rains more than 200 days a year here.

SCALE

0   250 miles

0   250 kilometers

Georgetown

Paramaribo

Cayenne

The heaviest spider in the world, this tarantula actually rarely eats birds. It prefers insects or earthworms.

GUYANA

Goliath birdeater

FRENCH GUIANA

SURINAME

ATLANTIC OCEAN

Found from Mexico to the top of Argentina, the harpy eagle has talons longer than a grizzly bear's claws.

Baby emerald tree boas are red or orange. They change to green as they grow up.

Emerald tree boa

Amazon

Harpy eagle

Tapajós

Piranhas are fierce predators with razor-sharp teeth, but insects and fish are their usual foods.

Madeira

Red-bellied piranha

Ring-tailed coati

Related to raccoons, coatis travel in groups of up to 65 individuals.

Army ant

Army ants form "swarm raids" of over 200,000 individuals, which kill any creature that can't move away.

BRAZIL

Araguaia

Tocantins

Electric eel

This long, snakelike fish has special organs that give an electric shock to prey.

Toco toucan

Tocos are the largest type of toucan. They use their big bills to pick and peel fruit.

Brasília

BOLIVIA

PARAGUAY

Red howler monkeys eat leaves and fruit.

Red howler monkey
Red howlers live up to their name. They are the loudest animals on land, and their howls can be heard 3 miles (5 km) away!

Jaguar
Jaguars are so good at hiding that scientists don't know how many exist in the wild. They are found throughout Central America and the northern half of South America.

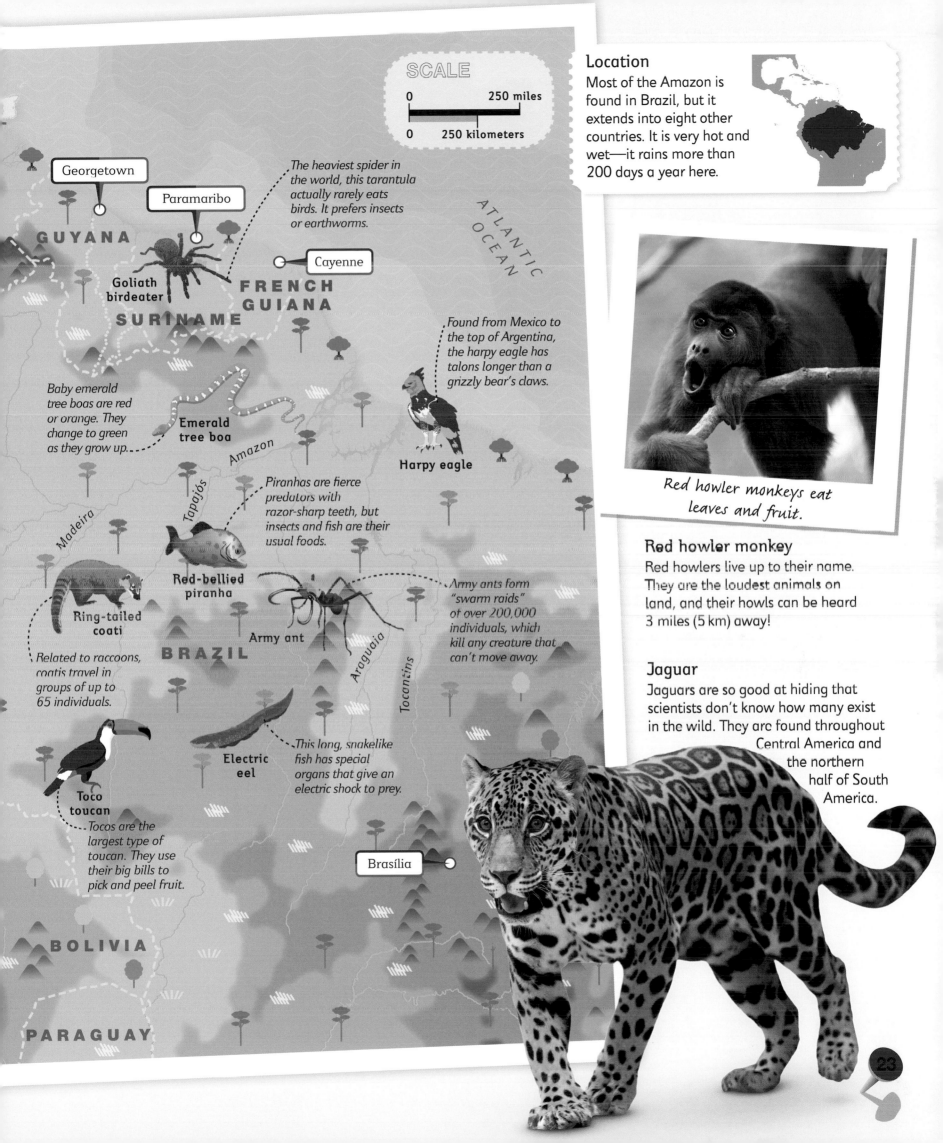

Andean mountains

The Andes mountain range is one of the highest in the world. It reaches a height of 22,831 ft (6,959 m) and stretches all along the west coast of South America. The animals here live in all kinds of habitats, from rocky peaks to tropical forests.

Peruvian firestick
The bright-red color of this stick insect warns predators to stay away. If threatened, it releases a nasty-smelling liquid.

The Peruvian firestick eats ferns.

Caracas

Orinoco

VENEZUELA

Milk snake

Found in mountain woodlands, this nonvenomous snake can grow to 6½ ft (2 m) long.

Magdalena

COLOMBIA

Bogotá

Spectacled bear

This is South America's only bear. It looks like it wears glasses because of the lighter-colored fur on its face.

Northern pudu

Quito

ECUADOR

The northern pudu is the tiniest deer in the world at just over 12 in (30 cm) tall.

Montane guinea pig

Lima

Also called a cavy, this wild guinea pig lives in groups in mountain grassland and forest edges.

Amazon

Madeira

BRAZIL

Only found in Lake Titicaca, this huge frog weighs up to 2.2 lb (1 kg) and breathes through its baggy skin.

PERU

ANDES

Trueb's cochran frog

The skin on this frog's belly is see-through—you can see its internal organs and even its bones!

These domestic animals live in groups in high mountain areas, where they eat hay, grass, and ferns.

Llama

BOLIVIA

Sucre

Lake Titicaca

Titicaca water frog

La Paz

James's flamingo

This pale-pink flamingo gets its color from the plantlike algae that it eats, which grow in high, salty lakes.

Location
The Andes stretch more than 4,500 miles (7,240 km) through seven countries. The climate here ranges from humid rain forest to snowy mountains.

Long-tailed chinchilla

With 60 hairs growing out of each follicle, this rodent has very thick fur. Having thick fur is ideal for the cold temperatures of the high Andes.

Caracaras often wander around, turning over stones to look for insects, rodents, and other animals to eat.

Mountain caracara

Colorado

Negro

Chubut

SOUTH ATLANTIC OCEAN

Falkland Islands

Also known as zorros, these foxlike wild dogs hunt lizards, insects, rabbits, and geese. They make their dens in rocky caves.

Culpeo

Santiago

Andean goose

A N D E S

Andean condor

CHILE

Huemul

This goose's blood absorbs more oxygen than other geese, so it can survive at high altitudes where there is less oxygen in the air.

PACIFIC OCEAN

The Andean condor is the world's largest flying bird. It rides mountain air currents with a wingspan of up to 10½ ft (3.2m).

Short legs allow this endangered deer to clamber over rough, high mountain terrain. It is the national animal of Chile.

HABITAT KEY

- Wetlands
- Deciduous forests
- Scrublands
- Mountains
- Temperate grasslands
- Cold desert
- Tropical grasslands

SCALE

0   250 miles

0   250 kilometers

The male cock of the rock can extend the crest on its head.

Andean cock of the rock

Male cock of the rocks are brilliant orange, while females are brownish. The males gather together to show off their feathers to females, who pick their favorite from the group.

Vicuña

These small members of the camel family are so well-adapted to their mountain homes that they can survive at altitudes as high as 16,404 ft (5,000 m).

Temperate pampas

With level plains as far as the eye can see, it's no wonder native South Americans named this region pampas—meaning "flat surface." This temperate grassland provides plenty of seeds for birds, insects, and small mammals to eat.

Eyes high on its head allow the coypu to see when it swims.

Coypu
Sometimes mistaken for a beaver, the coypu is a water-loving rodent that can get up to 3 ft (1 m) long. Also called the "nutria," it lives in riverside burrows and eats plants.

Argentine horned frog
At 5½ in (14 cm) long and weighing up to 1 lb (480 g), the horned frog is big enough to eat lizards, mice, and even other horned frogs.

This lizard gets up to 4½ ft (1.4 m) long. During the day it hunts for snails, spiders, and insects.

Argentine black and white teju

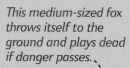

This bloodsucking bug feeds on rodents, marsupials, and even humans. It sometimes passes on a parasite that causes disease.

Assassin bug

SIERRAS DE CÓRDOBA

Desaguadero

This skunk uses its broad, fleshy nose to snuffle out beetles and spiders to eat.

Mollina's hog-nosed skunk

This medium-sized fox throws itself to the ground and plays dead if danger passes.

Pampas fox

ARGENTINA

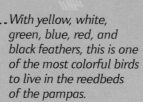

With yellow, white, green, blue, red, and black feathers, this is one of the most colorful birds to live in the reedbeds of the pampas.

Many-colored rush-tyrant

The greater rhea can reach 4½ ft (1.4 m) tall. It can't fly, but it can run as fast as 37 mph (60 kph).

Greater rhea

The long, powerful legs of this large rodent allow it to run up to 30 mph (48 kph).

Patagonian mara

Colorado

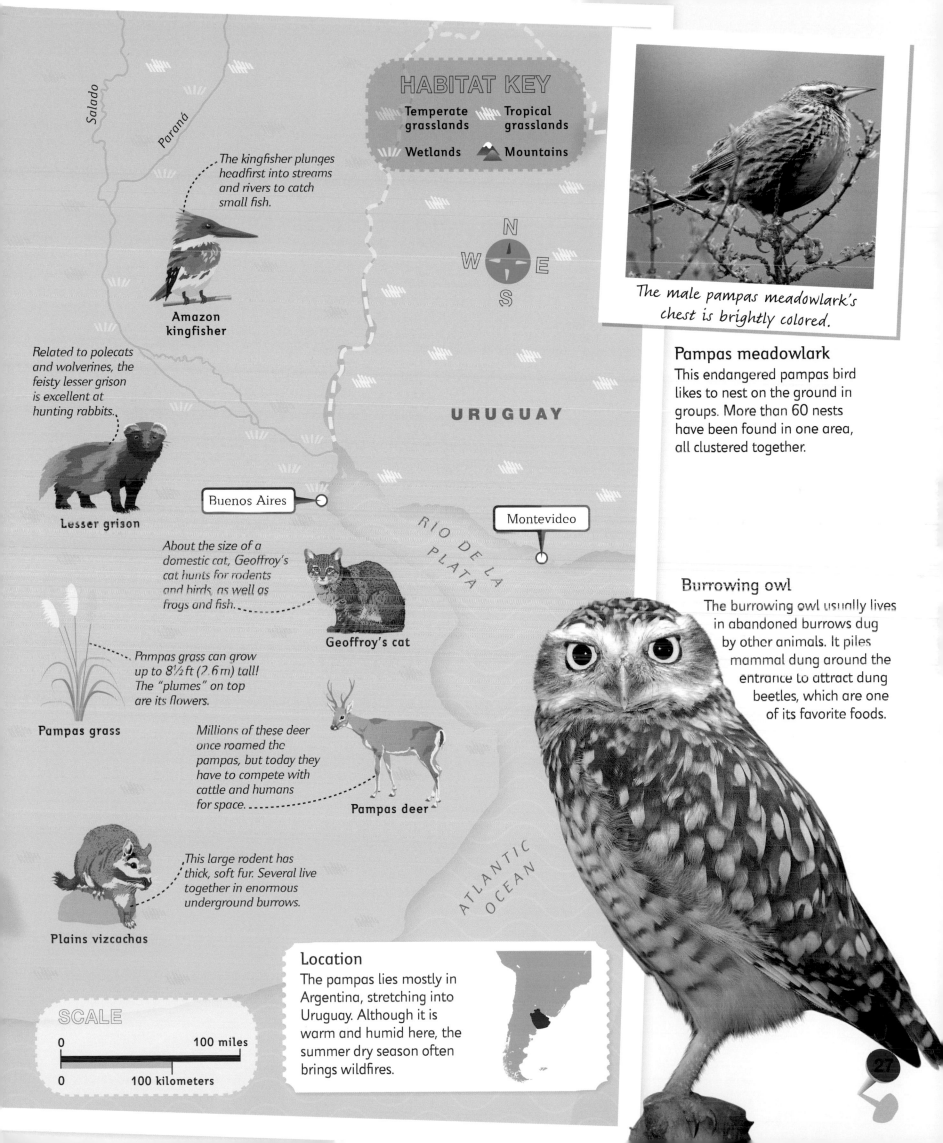

HABITAT KEY

Temperate grasslands

Tropical grasslands

Wetlands

Mountains

The kingfisher plunges headfirst into streams and rivers to catch small fish.

Amazon kingfisher

Salado

Paraná

Related to polecats and wolverines, the feisty lesser grison is excellent at hunting rabbits.

Lesser grison

URUGUAY

Buenos Aires

About the size of a domestic cat, Geoffroy's cat hunts for rodents and birds, as well as frogs and fish.

Geoffroy's cat

RIO DE LA PLATA

Montevideo

Pampas grass can grow up to 8½ ft (2.6 m) tall! The "plumes" on top are its flowers.

Pampas grass

Millions of these deer once roamed the pampas, but today they have to compete with cattle and humans for space.

Pampas deer

This large rodent has thick, soft fur. Several live together in enormous underground burrows.

Plains vizcachas

ATLANTIC OCEAN

The male pampas meadowlark's chest is brightly colored.

Pampas meadowlark
This endangered pampas bird likes to nest on the ground in groups. More than 60 nests have been found in one area, all clustered together.

Burrowing owl
The burrowing owl usually lives in abandoned burrows dug by other animals. It piles mammal dung around the entrance to attract dung beetles, which are one of its favorite foods.

Location
The pampas lies mostly in Argentina, stretching into Uruguay. Although it is warm and humid here, the summer dry season often brings wildfires.

SCALE

0	100 miles
0	100 kilometers

27

Pantanal

The Pantanal is the world's largest wetland, which means a lot of it is underwater for much of the year. The 3,500 different plant species that grow here make it an ideal home for lots of birds and mammals, including the capybara, which is a giant relative of the guinea pig.

Jabiru stork

The jabiru is the tallest flying bird in South and Central America, and can grow to over 3 ft (1 m) high. It grabs fish, frogs, and insects with its enormous bill.

A jabiru stork wades through the Pantanal.

This big freshwater snail grows up to 6 in (15 cm) long! It only comes out of the water at night to find food.

Channeled apple snail

About as big as a medium-sized dog, the capybara is the world's largest rodent.

Capybara

The roseate spoonbill sweeps its spoon-shaped bill from side to side to scoop up minnows—tiny freshwater fish.

Paraguay

HABITAT KEY

Tropical grasslands

Deciduous forests

Wetlands

Anacondas live in and out of water. They can be up to 29½ ft (9 m) long, but hide among water plants to surprise prey.

Green anaconda

BOLIVIA

BRAZIL

SCALE

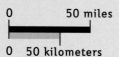

0   50 miles

0   50 kilometers

This wetland plant's leaves can grow to 8 ft (2.5 m) across, and can hold an animal weighing up to 45 lb (20.5 kg)!

Roseate spoonbill

The marsh deer has broad hooves that spread out to prevent them from sinking in marshy ground.

Marsh deer

Location

The Pantanal lies south of the Amazon rain forest in Brazil, Bolivia, and Paraguay. It gets so much rain that 80 percent of it is flooded during the rainy season.

This clever monkey uses rocks to crack nuts and crush crab shells to get at the food inside.

Hooded capuchin

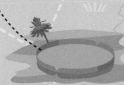

Giant water lily

PARAGUAY

Giant otter

Found only in South American rivers and rain forests, giant otters get up to 4½ ft (1.4 m) long. They eat fish, crabs, and even small caimans!

Yacare caiman

Caiman look like their alligator relatives, but have a pointier snout. The yacare gets up to 10 ft (3 m) long. Its favorite food is the piranha, but it also eats apple snails.

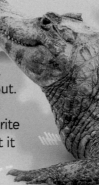

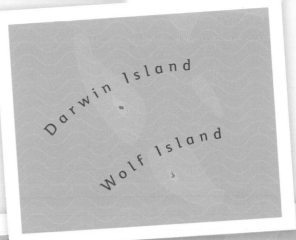

Darwin Island

Wolf Island

Galápagos

The Galápagos are a group of volcanic islands that lie about 621 miles (1,000 km) off the coast of Ecuador. There are several larger islands and many more smaller ones. Three major ocean currents meet here, bringing in lots of different sea animals.

Location
The Galápagos islands cluster around the equator in the Pacific Ocean. They have two seasons—a cool, dry season and a warm season.

PACIFIC OCEAN

Marchena Island

A marine iguana grazes on seaweed.

More lava lizards live in the Galápagos than any other reptile. They warm themselves on sunny rocks.

Although it can't fly, this cormorant is a powerful swimmer and hunts eels and octopuses on the ocean floor.

Galápagos lava lizard

Bright-blue feet make this bird easy to spot. Female boobies have darker-blue feet than males.

Blue-footed booby

Flightless cormorant

Fernandina Island

Galápagos hawk

San Salvador Island

Santa Cruz Island

Marine iguana
Marine iguanas are the only lizards to swim in the ocean, where they look for seaweed to eat. Special glands clean salt from their blood, which they sneeze out!

Galápagos sea lion

This little penguin lives farther north than any other penguin species.

Galápagos penguin

The Galápagos hawk is very rare. It mostly eats giant centipedes, but also catches rodents and young iguanas.

This sea lion can move its back flippers independently, so it can "gallop" on land.

San Cristóbal Island

Galápagos tortoise

This tortoise can grow up to 5 ft (1.5 m) long and weigh up to 500 lb (227 kg). Some of them are over 100 years old!

Isabela Island

Sally Lightfoot crab
This bright-red crab earned its name by scuttling around at high speeds. It hides from birds by squeezing into tiny spaces between rocks.

Santa María Island

Española Island

N W E S

SCALE

0   25 miles

0   25 kilometers

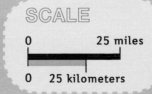

Cerrado

The Cerrado is found almost entirely in Brazil. It is made up of mostly tropical grassland, but a few trees are mixed with it in places, and there are areas of dry forest, too. With more than 10,000 different plant species, the Cerrado offers plenty of food and shelter for lots of animals.

HABITAT KEY

- Wetlands
- Tropical grasslands
- Mountains
- Tropical forests
- Deciduous forests
- Cold desert

Tapajós

Xing

Both male and female hyacinth macaws are bright blue.

Hyacinth macaw
The longest parrot on the planet, the hyacinth macaw can be 3 ft (1 m) long. Their large bills are able to crack even the hardest palm nuts.

Often called "a fox on stilts," the maned wolf's long legs help it to see over the tall Cerrado grass.

The giant anteater uses its sticky tongue to lap up 35,000 ants and termites a day!

Maned wolf

Giant anteater

King vultures don't have a great sense of smell. To make up for it, they follow other vultures to lead them to dead animals to eat.

King vulture

Boettger's caecilian

BOLIVIA

Although it has no legs, this isn't a snake, but an amphibian that lives underground.

Only the male helmeted manakin has this flashy red crest. The female is a plain gray-green bird.

Helmeted manakin

Found all over Central America and the north of South America, this lizard spends most of its life in trees, where it eats tender green leaves.

Green iguana

Leaf-cutting ants
These ants "saw" leaves into pieces with their jaws. They carry the bits back to their underground home, where a fungus grows on them, which the ants harvest and eat.

PARAGUAY

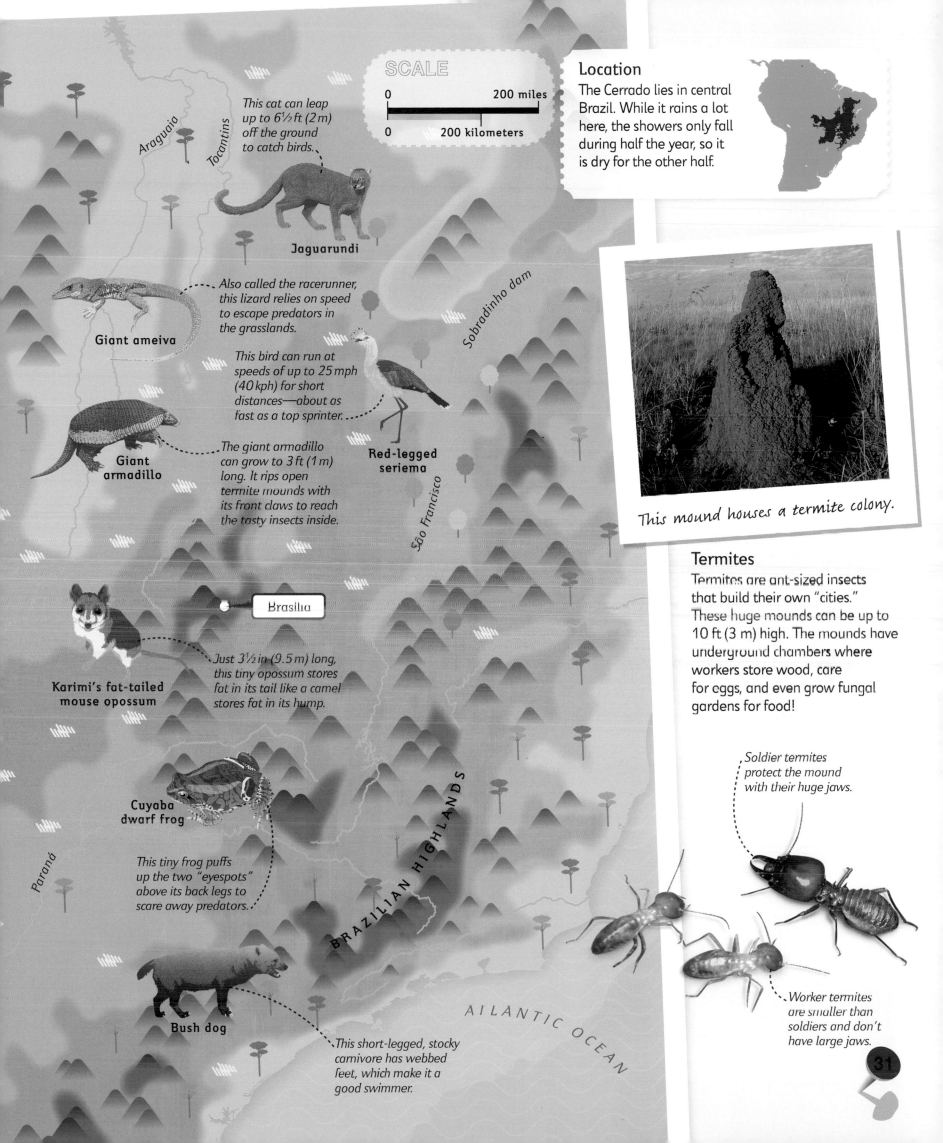

This cat can leap up to 6½ ft (2 m) off the ground to catch birds.

Jaguarundi

Also called the racerunner, this lizard relies on speed to escape predators in the grasslands.

Giant ameiva

This bird can run at speeds of up to 25 mph (40 kph) for short distances—about as fast as a top sprinter.

The giant armadillo can grow to 3 ft (1 m) long. It rips open termite mounds with its front claws to reach the tasty insects inside.

Giant armadillo

Red-legged seriema

Araguaia

Tocantins

Sobradinho dam

São Francisco

Karimi's fat-tailed mouse opossum

Just 3½ in (9.5 m) long, this tiny opossum stores fat in its tail like a camel stores fat in its hump.

Brasília

Cuyaba dwarf frog

This tiny frog puffs up the two "eyespots" above its back legs to scare away predators.

Paraná

BRAZILIAN HIGHLANDS

Bush dog

This short-legged, stocky carnivore has webbed feet, which make it a good swimmer.

ATLANTIC OCEAN

Location

The Cerrado lies in central Brazil. While it rains a lot here, the showers only fall during half the year, so it is dry for the other half.

This mound houses a termite colony.

Termites

Termites are ant-sized insects that build their own "cities." These huge mounds can be up to 10 ft (3 m) high. The mounds have underground chambers where workers store wood, care for eggs, and even grow fungal gardens for food!

Soldier termites protect the mound with their huge jaws.

Worker termites are smaller than soldiers and don't have large jaws.

31

Cordillera Blanca

Part of the Andes, this is the largest tropical mountain range in the world. Peaks over 19,685 ft (6,000 m) high surround valleys filled with lakes and streams. There isn't much oxygen at these heights, so it is hard to breathe, but the animals here manage surprisingly well.

Andean condor Female condors produce just one egg every two years. It takes almost 60 days for the egg to hatch.

Taruca

You can tell a taruca apart from other deer by the dark, Y-shaped mark on its face. It feeds on mountain grasses, and travels into valleys to find water.

Guanaco The guanaco is a member of the camel family. Movable pads on its hooves help it walk over rocky ground.

The guanaco is the ancestor of domestic llamas. The closely related vicuña is the ancestor of domestic alpacas.

Andean goose The Andean goose lives in mountain wetlands, but it doesn't swim well, so it avoids the water!

Colocolo The colocolo is a nocturnal predator that hunts rodents, guinea pigs, and ground-nesting birds.

Vizcachas are related to chinchillas.

Southern mountain vizcacha

The rabbitlike vizcacha spends a lot of time on rocky ledges, basking in the sun. It is covered in thick, soft fur all the way to the end of its curled tail.

The colocolo resembles a house cat, but can be identified by the dark-colored bands and lines around its legs.

Mountain caracara This black-and-white bird of prey builds nests of sticks on cliff ledges in the high Andes.

Torrent duck
Native to the Andes, the torrent duck plunges in and out of cold, fast-moving mountain streams to catch insect larvae to eat. Females, like this one, are orange, but males are black and white.

The spectacled bear lives only in the Andean mountains.

Spectacled bear The spectacled bear eats fruit, flowers, and plants. It also hunts insects, rodents, and birds in grassland habitats.

Culpeo The culpeo spends most of its time alone, but parents stay together to raise cubs in mountain dens.

Location
The Cordillera Blanca is a chain of mountains in northern Peru. Snow covers many of them, and temperatures range from 37–73°F (3–23°C).

Giant hummingbird
Giant hummingbirds get up to 8½ in (21.5 cm) long! They mostly feed on nectar from flowers, looking for the ones with the highest levels of energy-filled sugar. They also eat spiders and small insects.

Giant hummingbirds are the biggest hummingbirds in the world.

Africa

This continent is so large and has so many different habitats, it feels as if there are several Africas, not just one. With deserts and rain forests, mountains and grasslands, Africa is home to some of the best-known—and most endangered—species on Earth.

African savanna

Africa's tropical grassland is known as savanna. It is often what people think of when they imagine Africa: vast, open, grassy plains. Lots of hoofed animals live here, moving around in search of fresh grass—or, in the giraffe's case, tender acacia leaves to eat.

South African fynbos

The southwest tip of South Africa is covered with shrubs and heathland known as fynbos. Animals such as tortoises, frogs, and small baboons live among the 9,000 plant species that grow here.

Canary Islands (SPAIN)

MOROCCO

ALGERIA

TUNISIA

WESTERN SAHARA

MAURITANIA

MALI

NIGER

CAPE VERDE

SENEGAL

THE GAMBIA

GUINEA-BISSAU

GUINEA

BURKINA FASO

SIERRA LEONE

ATLANTIC OCEAN

LIBERIA

IVORY COAST

GHANA

TOGO

BENIN

NIGERIA

CAMEROON

GULF OF GUINEA

Bioco

EQUATORIAL GUINEA

São Tomé & Príncipe

GABON

CONGO

N
W E
S

HABITAT KEY

- Tropical forests
- Deciduous forests
- Coniferous forests
- Tropical grasslands
- Scrublands
- Deserts
- Wetlands
- Mountains
- Mangroves

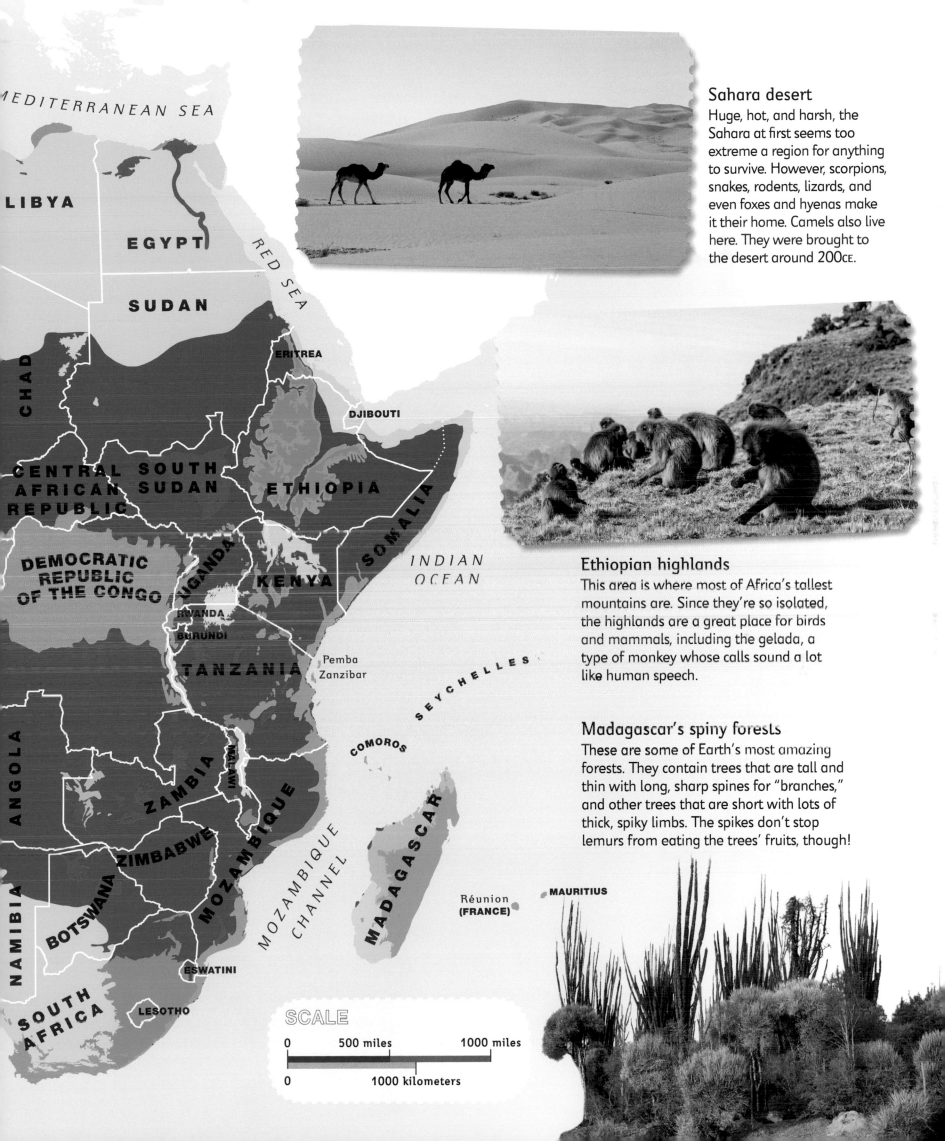

Sahara desert

Huge, hot, and harsh, the Sahara at first seems too extreme a region for anything to survive. However, scorpions, snakes, rodents, lizards, and even foxes and hyenas make it their home. Camels also live here. They were brought to the desert around 200CE.

Ethiopian highlands

This area is where most of Africa's tallest mountains are. Since they're so isolated, the highlands are a great place for birds and mammals, including the gelada, a type of monkey whose calls sound a lot like human speech.

Madagascar's spiny forests

These are some of Earth's most amazing forests. They contain trees that are tall and thin with long, sharp spines for "branches," and other trees that are short with lots of thick, spiky limbs. The spikes don't stop lemurs from eating the trees' fruits, though!

MEDITERRANEAN SEA

LIBYA

EGYPT

RED SEA

SUDAN

CHAD

ERITREA

DJIBOUTI

CENTRAL AFRICAN REPUBLIC

SOUTH SUDAN

ETHIOPIA

SOMALIA

DEMOCRATIC REPUBLIC OF THE CONGO

UGANDA

KENYA

INDIAN OCEAN

RWANDA

BURUNDI

TANZANIA

Pemba
Zanzibar

SEYCHELLES

ANGOLA

ZAMBIA

MALAWI

COMOROS

NAMIBIA

ZIMBABWE

MOZAMBIQUE

MOZAMBIQUE CHANNEL

MADAGASCAR

Réunion (FRANCE)

MAURITIUS

BOTSWANA

ESWATINI

LESOTHO

SOUTH AFRICA

SCALE

0   500 miles   1000 miles

0   1000 kilometers

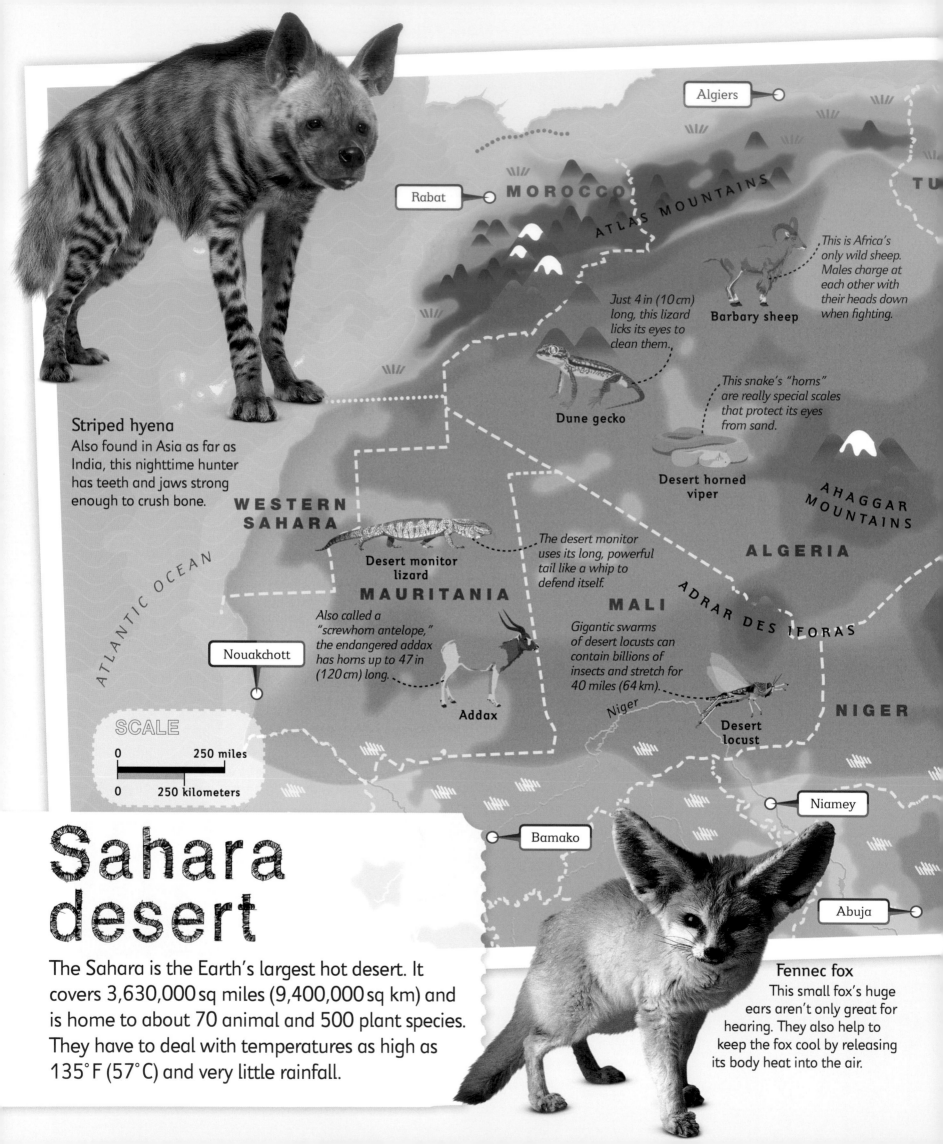

Algiers

Rabat

MOROCCO

ATLAS MOUNTAINS

Barbary sheep
This is Africa's only wild sheep. Males charge at each other with their heads down when fighting.

Just 4 in (10 cm) long, this lizard licks its eyes to clean them.

Dune gecko

This snake's "horns" are really special scales that protect its eyes from sand.

Desert horned viper

AHAGGAR MOUNTAINS

Striped hyena
Also found in Asia as far as India, this nighttime hunter has teeth and jaws strong enough to crush bone.

WESTERN SAHARA

ALGERIA

Desert monitor lizard

The desert monitor uses its long, powerful tail like a whip to defend itself.

MAURITANIA

MALI

ADRAR DES IFORAS

Also called a "screwhorn antelope," the endangered addax has horns up to 47 in (120 cm) long.

Nouakchott

Gigantic swarms of desert locusts can contain billions of insects and stretch for 40 miles (64 km).

Niger

NIGER

Addax

Desert locust

SCALE

0 ——— 250 miles

0 ——— 250 kilometers

Niamey

Bamako

Abuja

Sahara desert

The Sahara is the Earth's largest hot desert. It covers 3,630,000 sq miles (9,400,000 sq km) and is home to about 70 animal and 500 plant species. They have to deal with temperatures as high as 135°F (57°C) and very little rainfall.

ATLANTIC OCEAN

Fennec fox
This small fox's huge ears aren't only great for hearing. They also help to keep the fox cool by releasing its body heat into the air.

Tunis

N W E S

MEDITERRANEAN SEA

SIA

Tripoli

Cairo

EGYPT

This scorpion's venom is highly toxic, and it can be fatal to humans.

This crocodile gets up to 20 ft (6 m) long, weighs 2,205 lb (1,000 kg), and lives up to 40 years.

Deathstalker scorpion

LIBYA

The tiny hopping jerboa's hind legs are four times longer than its front ones.

Nile crocodile

Nile

RED SEA

Lesser Egyptian jerboa

Sandy-colored markings make it easy for this bird to hide from desert predators.

Found in southern desert shrubland, the Nubian bustard eats large insects, leaves, fruit, and grass seeds.

TIBESTI MOUNTAINS

A Ï R   M O U N T A I N S

The Dorcas gazelle never has to drink. It gets all its moisture from eating flowers, leaves, and bark.

The largest tortoise in Africa, this reptile can weigh up to 231 lbs (105 kg)

Dorcas gazelle

Chestnut-bellied sandgrouse

ERITREA

African spurred tortoise

Khartoum

Asmara

Nubian bustard

CHAD

SUDAN

ETHIOPIA

N'Djamena

NIGERIA

Chari

Location

The Sahara stretches across North Africa, from the Atlantic Ocean in the west all the way to the Red Sea in the east.

Dromedary camel

Dromedaries are well suited to the desert. They can store fat in their hump as food, have thick eyelashes to keep sand out of their eyes, and can drink 40 gallons (182 liters) of water without stopping!

Dromedary camels have only one hump.

Congo Basin

Often called "Africa's Green Heart," the Congo Basin is a huge area of land surrounding the Congo River. This supports the world's second-largest rain forest, and, along with swamps and lakes, it is a haven for hundreds of amazing animals—including bonobos and chimpanzees, the closest living relatives of humans.

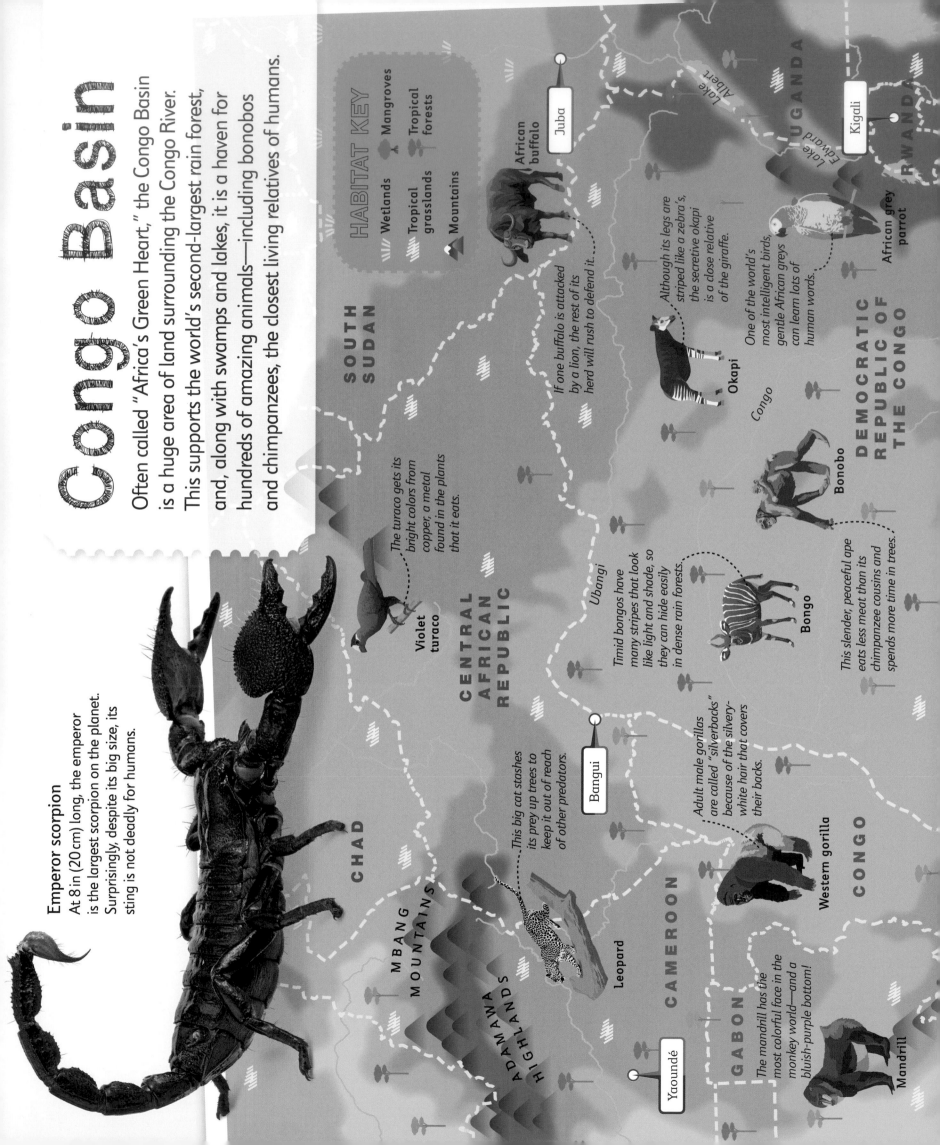

Emperor scorpion

At 8 in (20 cm) long, the emperor is the largest scorpion on the planet. Surprisingly, despite its big size, its sting is not deadly for humans.

HABITAT KEY

- ≋ Wetlands
- ≋ Tropical grasslands
- ▲ Mountains
- ⌂ Mangroves
- ⌂ Tropical forests

African buffalo

If one buffalo is attacked by a lion, the rest of its herd will rush to defend it.

Okapi

Although its legs are striped like a zebra's, the secretive okapi is a close relative of the giraffe.

African grey parrot

One of the world's most intelligent birds, gentle African greys can learn lots of human words.

Bonobo

This slender, peaceful ape eats less meat than its chimpanzee cousins and spends more time in trees.

Violet turaco

The turaco gets its bright colors from copper, a metal found in the plants that it eats.

Bongo

Timid bongos have many stripes that look like light and shade, so they can hide easily in dense rain forests.

Leopard

This big cat stashes its prey up trees to keep it out of reach of other predators.

Western gorilla

Adult male gorillas are called "silverbacks" because of the silvery-white hair that covers their backs.

Mandrill

The mandrill has the most colorful face in the monkey world—and a bluish-purple bottom!

SOUTH SUDAN

CENTRAL AFRICAN REPUBLIC

DEMOCRATIC REPUBLIC OF THE CONGO

CHAD

CAMEROON

GABON

CONGO

UGANDA

RWANDA

MBANG MOUNTAINS

ADAMAWA HIGHLANDS

Lake Albert

Lake Edward

Congo

Ubangi

Juba

Bangui

Yaoundé

Kigali

BURUNDI

TANZANIA

Lake Tanganyika

MITUMBA MOUNTAINS

Common pangolin

Covered in protective scales, the pangolin rolls itself into a ball when threatened.

African fish eagle

This eagle swoops down on fish from nearby trees, grabbing them in its sharp talons.

Congo

ZAMBIA

Kasai

This tiny bloodsucker causes more deaths than any other creature because it passes on the disease malaria.

Anopheles mosquito

ANGOLA

Kinshasa

Brazzaville

Slender lungfish

The lungfish lives in floodplains that often dry up. During these times, it uses its lungs to breathe air until the water returns.

ATLANTIC OCEAN

Luanda

N
W E
S

SCALE

0   200 miles

0   200 kilometers

Location

The Congo Basin is located around the equator in west-central Africa. There are hot, humid places, and cooler, dry ones. Some parts also get a lot of rain.

The red river hog uses its snout to sniff out tasty roots in the ground.

Chimpanzee

This smart ape lives in family groups and can walk on two legs as well as four. It uses tools, such as rocks and sticks, to help it get food.

Red river hog

Red river hogs move around mostly at night, returning to burrows during the day to keep cool. They live in noisy family groups called sounders.

Chimpanzees are one of the closest living relatives of humans.

White-throated bee-eater

The bee-eater lives in large families. It rubs bees and wasps against a hard surface to remove their stings before eating them.

Southern savanna

Much of southern Africa is covered in tropical grasslands called savanna. They're great places to find grazing animals, such as zebras and antelopes. This also means that they attract predators, such as lions.

DEMOCRATIC REPUBLIC OF THE CONGO

Kinda baboon babies can have white, gray, black, or even multicolored fur.

Kinda baboon

"Hippopotamus" means "water horse," but the hippo's closest relatives are dolphins and whales!

Hippopotamus

HABITAT KEY

\\\|/ Wetlands

\\\|/ Tropical grasslands

🌳 Mangroves

⛰ Mountains

🌳 Deciduous forests

🌲 Tropical forests

▨ Hot desert

SCALE

```
0        100 miles
0        100 kilometers
```

BIÉ PLATEAU

This tree-dwelling primate, also called a bush baby, can jump as far as 16 ft (5 m) in a single leap.

Mohol galago

Zambezi

ANGOLA

Lions are social cats. They live in groups called prides.

African lion

African elephant

Earth's largest land animal, the African elephant has a brain four times bigger than a human brain.

These dogs help each other. They rarely fight, and they take care of young, old, sick, or injured members of their pack.

ATLANTIC OCEAN

Rhinoceroses don't see very well, but they have good hearing and an excellent sense of smell.

BOTSWANA

African wild dog

Okavango

Black rhinoceros

NAMIBIA

Grant's zebra

Just like human fingerprints, a zebra's stripe pattern is unique. This means that no two zebras have the exact same stripes.

Location

Savanna covers more than half of Africa, mostly in the central and southern parts. These areas have a rainy and a dry season, but it is hot all year.

TANZANIA

MITUMBA MOUNTAINS

Lake Tanganyika

Male impalas grow beautiful ridged horns up to 36 in (92 cm) long.

Impala

Vervet monkeys spend hours each day picking dirt and parasites out of each other's fur.

ZAMBIA

MALAWI

Lake Nyasa

MUCHINGA MOUNTAINS

Vervet monkey

Lilongwe

One of the few savanna trees, the acacia provides food for many animals—despite its fierce thorns.

Acacia tree

MOZAMBIQUE

Lusaka

Zambezi

Southern yellow-billed hornbill

This bird snaps up insects with its curved bill, tossing them into its mouth with a flick of its head.

INYANGA MOUNTAINS

Long-legged flamingos sweep their bills through salty water to find algae to eat.

Lesser flamingo

MOZAMBIQUE CHANNEL

Harare

N
W   E
S

Plum dung beetle

Dung beetles recycle animal poop. They roll it up into balls and bury them to use later as food or as places to lay eggs.

ZIMBABWE

INDIAN OCEAN

Giraffe

At up to 19 ft (5.8 m) high, the giraffe is the world's tallest land animal. Its very long neck helps it to reach acacia tree leaves high above the savanna.

Blue wildebeest

The wildebeest looks like a cow, but it is a type of antelope. It travels an astonishing 1,000 miles (1,609 km) every year, just to find the right kind of grass to eat.

Wildebeests are also known as gnus.

41

Kalahari desert

The Kalahari is a huge, dry, sandy area in southern Africa. In some parts of the Kalahari, it may not rain for up to eight months. Many animals here have to travel in search of fresh grass to eat, and predators follow them.

Sociable weaver
These small birds build giant nests, over 21 ft (6 m) wide, with up to 100 weavers in each one. Some nests are so heavy that they break the tree they're in!

Sociable weavers' massive nests can last for 100 years.

HABITAT KEY
- Wetlands
- Scrublands
- Tropical grasslands
- Hot desert

SCALE
0   100 miles

0   100 kilometers

ANGOLA

Okavango

Circling high in the desert sky on its broad wings, this bird searches for dead animals to eat.

Location
The Kalahari covers most of Botswana and parts of Namibia and South Africa. In summer, it can become as hot as 104°F (40°C).

White-backed vulture

Growing up to 9 ft (2.8 m) tall, the ostrich is the world's largest bird. It can't fly, but it can outrun most of its predators.

Springbok

This high-leaping antelope moves around in large herds. Both males and females have horns.

BOTSWANA

Ostrich

Warthogs kneel on their front legs when munching on fresh grass.

 Windhoek

The aardvark's name means "earth pig." It can eat up to 50,000 ants a night!

Aardvark

Common warthog

During the day, this large rodent sleeps in caves or burrows. At night, it comes out to find plants to eat.

NAMIBIA

N W E S

Cheetah
The world's fastest land animal, the cheetah can run at speeds of up to 68 mph (110 kph). It takes just three seconds for this cat to reach its top speed.

Gaborone

Pretoria

Cape porcupine

African bullfrog

This big frog lives underground during the dry season, which can last 10 months of each year!

Vaal

Bloemfontein

SOUTH AFRICA

Meerkat
Meerkats help each other protect their families. They take turns standing on guard and warn other meerkats if danger approaches.

Madagascar

Madagascar is the fourth-largest island in the world, and it is amazingly rich in wildlife. More than 250,000 different species of animals live here, and two-thirds of them are found nowhere else on Earth. Sadly, many are endangered.

Location

Madagascar is in the Indian Ocean, off the coast of Africa. It has two seasons: hot and rainy, and then cool and dry.

Male panther chameleons are color crazy! Their body patterns are a mix of pink, blue, orange, green, red, and yellow.

Panther chameleon

MOZAMBIQUE CHANNEL

INDIAN OCEAN

Male ploughshare tortoises try to flip each other over during fights.

MADAGASCAR

Ploughshare tortoise

Betsiboka

The baobab's thick, wide trunk can hold thousands of liters of rainwater.

Lake Alaotra

Tomato frog

This frog's bright-red color is a warning to predators that it is toxic.

Antananarivo

Leaf chameleon

Just 1.1 in (29 mm) long, this tiny species of leaf chameleon remained unknown to scientists until 2012.

This hedgehoglike animal has spines sticking out of its fur.

Baobab

Lowland streaked tenrec

ANKARATRA MASSIF

Leaf chameleons are possibly the world's smallest reptile.

HABITAT KEY

- Mangroves
- Mountains
- Tropical forests
- Deciduous forests

Mangoky

This strange-looking lemur taps its long middle finger on trees to find grubs—its favorite food.

The ring-tailed lemur sunbathes every morning with its arms outstretched.

Aye-aye

Fossa

Madagascar's largest predator is the catlike fossa. It climbs trees and uses its long tail to help it balance. Fossas hunt many animals, from lemurs to fish.

Comet moth

The comet moth is also called the Madagascan moon moth. It has a wingspan of 8 in (20 cm) and its striking tail is 6 in (15 cm) long. The adult moth lives for just a few days.

Ring-tailed lemur

Kruger National Park

South Africa's Kruger National Park is filled with wildlife. More than 140 mammal species and hundreds of birds live in its savanna, mountains, and tropical forests. Watering holes provide places for animals to drink during the dry season.

The white-backed vulture is the most commonly seen vulture in Africa.

White-backed vulture
This big vulture eats dead animals. Hundreds of them may gather to feed on a carcass, squabbling and fighting while they eat!

Giraffe Special valves in a giraffe's neck stop blood from rushing to its head when it bends over to drink.

Hippopotamus A hippo's eyes, ears, and nose are on top of its head, so it can see, hear, and breathe while the rest of it is underwater.

Honey badger Almost 3 ft (1 m) long, the honey badger is one of the most fearless animals in Africa. It even fights lions!

Aardvark The aardvark uses its wide, strong claws to dig burrows as well as find insects to eat.

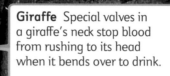

The aardvark's nostrils contain lots of hairs to stop dust from going up its nose when it is digging.

Secretary bird
The secretary bird strides through the savanna on its long legs, looking for grasshoppers, voles, and mice to eat. It kills snakes by stomping on them!

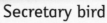

Bateleur
This eagle's name means "tightrope walker" because it rocks its wings from side to side when it glides, as if it's balancing. Its bright-red face has no feathers at all.

Plains zebra Zebra herds travel long distances to find enough grass to eat. They must also drink at least once a day.

African elephant An elephant's trunk contains 40,000 muscles! It uses its trunk to spray water into its mouth for a drink.

African elephants have much larger ears than Asian elephants.

African lion In a pride of lions, females do most of the hunting. The male is the only cat with a mane.

Impala To escape predators, impalas leap forward up to 29½ ft (9 m) and as high as 8 ft (2.5 m). Sometimes they leap over each other!

Impalas eat grass in the rainy season and shrubs and herbs at other times.

Location
Kruger National Park covers 7,523 sq miles (19,485 sq km) in northeastern South Africa. It lies south of Zimbabwe and west of Mozambique.

Cheetah
A cheetah's impressive bursts of speed can only last for short distances. Afterward, it's tired, so other animals can easily steal its kill!

Cheetahs are instantly recognizable from the black spots on their coat.

45

Europe

At first glance, the continent of Europe may seem too crowded for wildlife. There are 748 million people living here, in 44 countries! But with dense forests, sandy beaches, high mountains, and miles of moorland, animals still have plenty of different habitats to choose from.

HABITAT KEY

HABITAT KEY

Deciduous forests

Coniferous forests

Scrublands

Temperate grasslands

Deserts

Tundra

Ice

Scottish moorland
Northern Scotland has acres of moorland. These rainy highlands have acidic, peaty soil, formed by sphagnum moss. They are full of a pretty pink- and purple-flowering shrub called heather. Heather is home to many insects, birds, and small mammals.

The Camargue
This triangular coastal wetland is found where the Rhône River meets the Mediterranean Sea. Its 359 sq miles (930 sq km) of sandy marshes are home to 400 bird species, and to animals unique to this area, such as the Camargue horse.

ICELAND

ATLANTIC OCEAN

Faroe Islands

NORWEGIAN SEA

Shetland Islands

NORTH SEA

NORWAY

SWEDEN

DENMARK

Bornholm

IRELAND

Isle of Man

UNITED KINGDOM

NETHERLANDS

GERMANY

Channel Islands

BELGIUM

LUXEMBOURG

CZECH REPUBLIC

BAY OF BISCAY

FRANCE

LIECHTENSTEIN

SWITZERLAND

AUSTRIA

SLOVENIA

Azores

SAN MARINO

CROATIA

ADRIATIC SEA

PORTUGAL

ANDORRA

MONACO

SPAIN

Corsica

ITALY

Majorca

Minorca

VATICAN CITY

Ibiza

Sardinia

TYRRHENIAN SEA

Balearic Islands

Gibraltar

MEDITERRANEAN SEA

Sicily

Madeira

MALTA

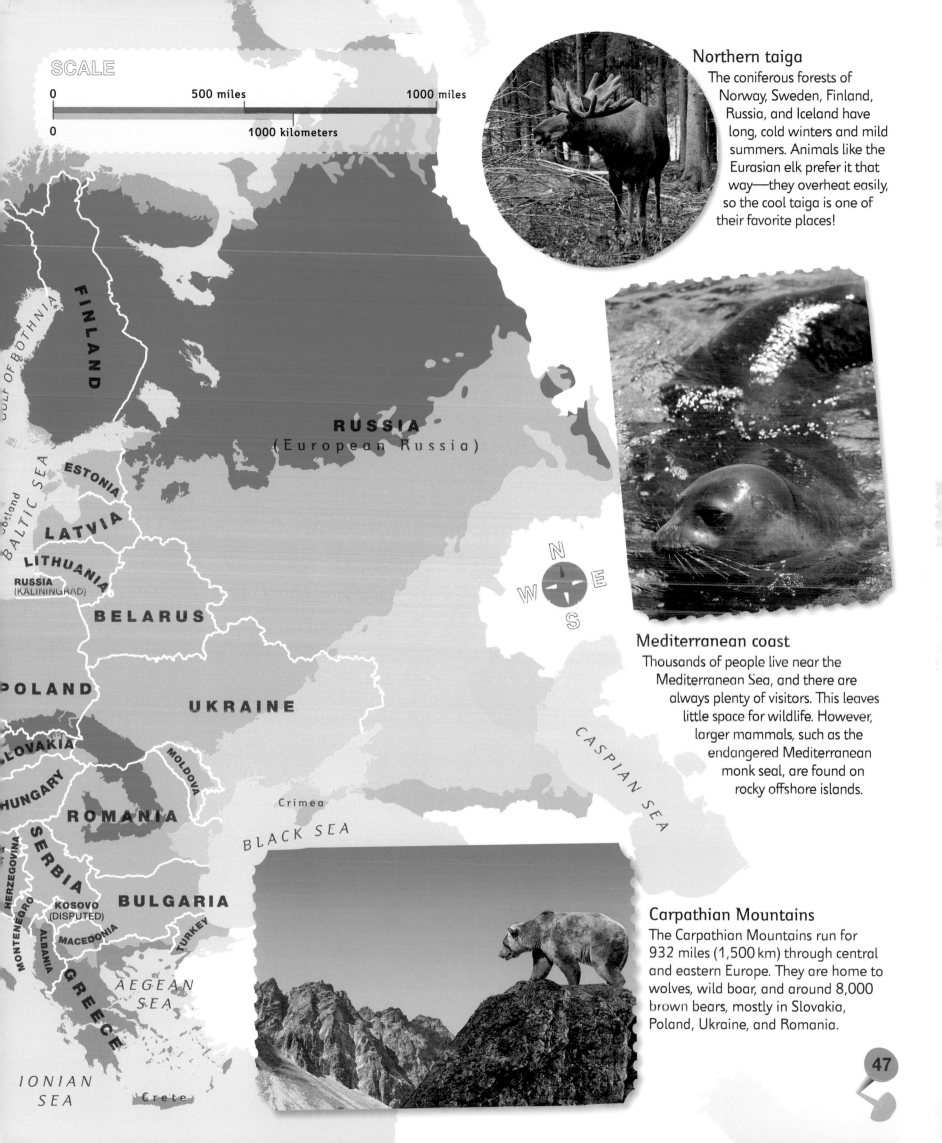

SCALE

| 0 | 500 miles | 1000 miles |

| 0 | 1000 kilometers |

GULF OF BOTHNIA

FINLAND

RUSSIA
(European Russia)

BALTIC SEA

Gotland

ESTONIA

LATVIA

LITHUANIA

RUSSIA
(KALININGRAD)

BELARUS

POLAND

UKRAINE

SLOVAKIA

HUNGARY

MOLDOVA

ROMANIA

Crimea

SERBIA

HERZEGOVINA

MONTENEGRO

ALBANIA

KOSOVO
(DISPUTED)

MACEDONIA

BULGARIA

BLACK SEA

TURKEY

GREECE

AEGEAN SEA

IONIAN SEA

Crete

CASPIAN SEA

Northern taiga
The coniferous forests of Norway, Sweden, Finland, Russia, and Iceland have long, cold winters and mild summers. Animals like the Eurasian elk prefer it that way—they overheat easily, so the cool taiga is one of their favorite places!

Mediterranean coast
Thousands of people live near the Mediterranean Sea, and there are always plenty of visitors. This leaves little space for wildlife. However, larger mammals, such as the endangered Mediterranean monk seal, are found on rocky offshore islands.

Carpathian Mountains
The Carpathian Mountains run for 932 miles (1,500 km) through central and eastern Europe. They are home to wolves, wild boar, and around 8,000 brown bears, mostly in Slovakia, Poland, Ukraine, and Romania.

47

Puffins can fly at about 55 mph (88 kph) and swim underwater for up to one minute.

Puffins

Reykjavík

ICELAND

NORWEGIAN SEA

In the spring, several male hares chase a female, who may turn around and box them with her front feet!

FINLAND

Mountain hare

Predators hunt many of these small rodents, but their numbers grow quickly. Females can have young every 3 to 4 weeks, all year round!

SWEDEN

This bat has shaggy brown fur with blond tips. It is the only bat found north of the Arctic Circle.

A superb climber, the lynx often hides in trees and then drops down onto an unsuspecting deer.

Northern bat

Norway lemming

N W E S

The boreal owl has such good hearing that it can pinpoint voles hidden beneath the snow.

Eurasian lynx

Boreal owl

NORWAY

Oslo

Helsinki

Stockholm

Tallinn

ESTONIA

Gotland

Riga

BALTIC SEA

LATVIA

LITHUANIA

BELARUS

Northern European taiga

Taiga is the evergreen forest that grows in cool, wet, mountainous places in the far north of the world. Mammals need thick, furry coats, and birds need to fluff up their feathers to keep warm. During the cold winters, food can be hard to find.

Carrion crow
The crow has a huge brain for its size. It's so smart that it makes and uses tools, and recognizes faces. It will even teach other crows to identify a mean human!

BARENTS SEA

This type of finch's bill is crossed at the tip, which is ideal for pulling conifer seeds out of cones.

Parrot crossbill

The eider swallows mussels whole, crushing their shells in its stomach.

Common eider
The eider is the Northern Hemisphere's largest duck. Mother eiders lead their chicks to the sea, where they swim in groups of more than 150 chicks!

The wolverine is the biggest member of the weasel family. It has a bite so powerful it can crush bone.

Used as Christmas trees, the Norway spruce can grow to 131 ft (40 m) in height and live for 1,000 years.

The osprey plunges into water feetfirst to grab fish with its talons.

Osprey

Wolverine

RUSSIAN FEDERATION

Norway spruce

Northern Dvina

The jay survives cold winters by storing food, especially berries. It hides them in trees, or covers them with bark and lichens.

SCALE
0 — 100 miles

0 — 100 kilometers

Lake Onega

Male capercaillies perform a dance in an area called a "lek" to attract females. They put their tails up, their wings down, and make sounds like popping corks!

Sukhoma

Siberian jay

HABITAT KEY
▲ Mountains ▲ Coniferous forests
● Deciduous forests

Western capercaillie

This toad's skin gives off a nasty substance that stops most predators from eating it. It can live for up to 40 years.

Common toad

Stoat
The stoat is a lightning-fast member of the weasel family. Usually reddish brown, its coat turns white in winter, making it hard to see against the snow. The tip of its tail, however, stays dark.

Location
This part of the taiga runs across the top of Europe eastward to the Ural Mountains in western Russia. Winters here are very cold and snowy.

When a stoat has its white coat, it's called an ermine.

49

British Isles

The British Isles are made up of the United Kingdom—which includes England, Scotland, Wales, and Northern Ireland—and the Republic of Ireland. Although wolves and bears once lived here, today the largest wild mammal is a deer.

European badger

The badger likes to live in groups. Six or more share a system of underground tunnels called a sett, which they dig out with powerful claws. One badger can eat hundreds of earthworms in a single night!

European hedgehog

If threatened, this hedgehog curls up into a ball. Although it is known for eating earthworms and slugs, it actually prefers insects—even wasps and bees.

The European hedgehog has around 5,000 spines in its coat.

Red squirrels can be right- or left-handed—you can tell by the way they handle a pinecone.

Red squirrel

This wildcat looks like a big domestic cat, but it's really a fierce, strong predator with 18 razor-sharp claws!

Scottish wildcat

Cold British waters don't bother this marine mammal. It has a 2½ in (6 cm) layer of fat under its skin, called blubber, to keep it warm.

Gray seal

NORTH SEA

Shetland Islands

Orkney Islands

Inner Hebrides

Outer Hebrides

ATLANTIC OCEAN

GRAMPIANS

Edinburgh

Clyde

Scotland

SCALE

```
0        50 miles
0        50 kilometers
```

HABITAT KEY

- Wetlands
- Mountains
- Coniferous forests
- Deciduous forests

Location

This group of islands is found off the northwest coast of mainland Europe. The weather is often wet and windy, but summers can also be very warm.

N E S W

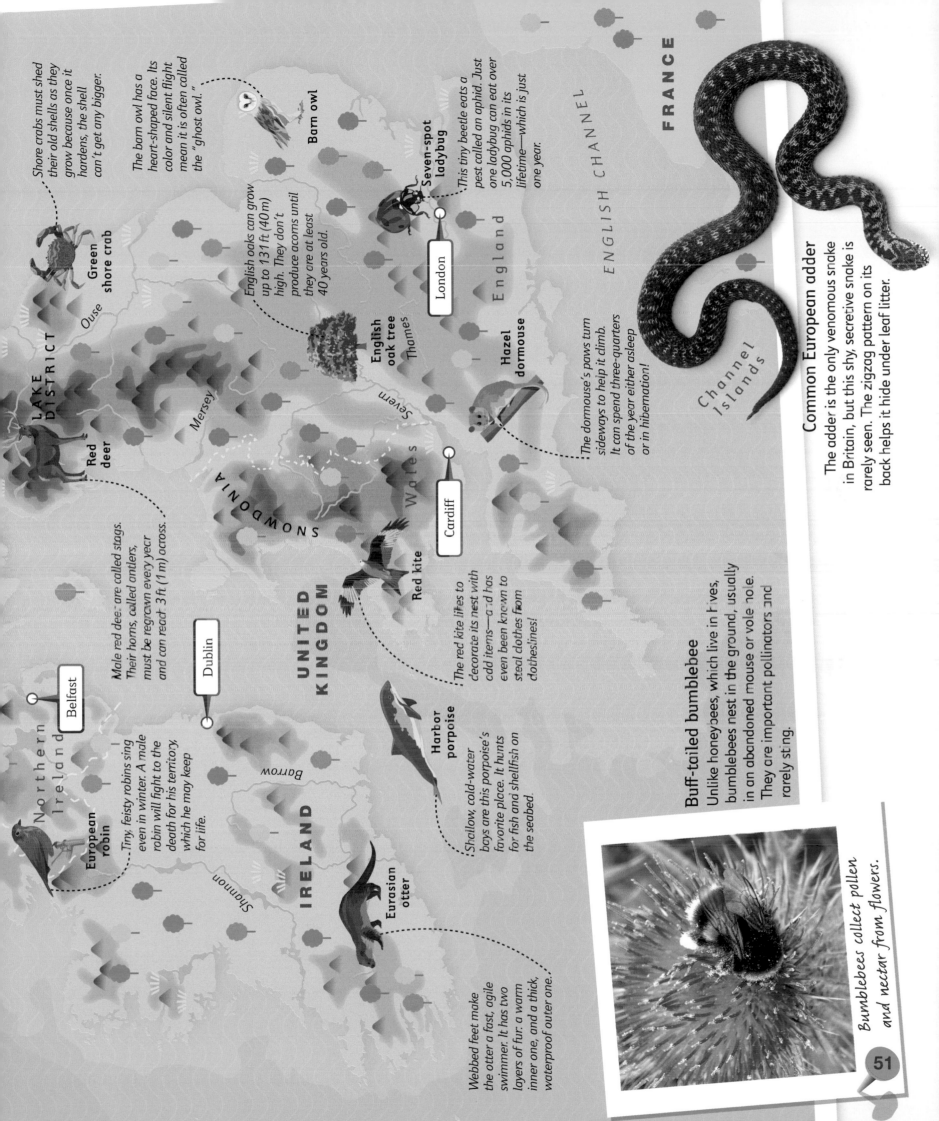

Shore crabs must shed their old shells as they grow because once it hardens, the shell can't get any bigger.

Green shore crab

Ouse

LAKE DISTRICT

Mersey

Red deer

Male red deer are called stags. Their horns, called antlers, must be regrown every year and can reach 3 ft (1 m) across.

Belfast

Northern Ireland

European robin

Tiny, feisty robins sing even in winter. A male robin will fight to the death for his territory, which he may keep for life.

Dublin

Shannon

Barrow

IRELAND

Eurasian otter

Webbed feet make the otter a fast, agile swimmer. It has two layers of fur: a warm inner one, and a thick, waterproof outer one.

UNITED KINGDOM

The barn owl has a heart-shaped face. Its color and silent flight mean it is often called the "ghost owl."

Barn owl

English oaks can grow up to 131 ft (40 m) high. They don't produce acorns until they are at least 40 years old.

English oak tree

Thames

SNOWDONIA

Cardiff

Red kite

The red kite likes to decorate its nest with odd items—and has even been known to steal clothes from clotheslines!

Severn

Wales

England

Seven-spot ladybug

This tiny beetle eats a pest called an aphid. Just one ladybug can eat over 5,000 aphids in its lifetime—which is just one year.

London

Hazel dormouse

The dormouse's paws turn sideways to help it climb. It can spend three-quarters of the year either asleep or in hibernation!

Harbor porpoise

Shallow, cold-water bays are this porpoise's favorite place. It hunts for fish and shellfish on the seabed.

ENGLISH CHANNEL

Channel Islands

FRANCE

Common European adder

The adder is the only venomous snake in Britain, but this shy, secretive snake is rarely seen. The zigzag pattern on its back helps it hide under leaf litter.

Buff-tailed bumblebee

Unlike honeybees, which live in hives, bumblebees nest in the ground, usually in an abandoned mouse or vole hole. They are important pollinators and rarely sting.

Bumblebees collect pollen and nectar from flowers.

51

European forests

Forests here mostly have a mix of trees. Some, like the Bavarian Forest in Germany, have more conifers, such as spruce. Others, such as Białowieża Forest in Poland, have more broad-leaved trees, like oak. All, however, provide great homes for animals.

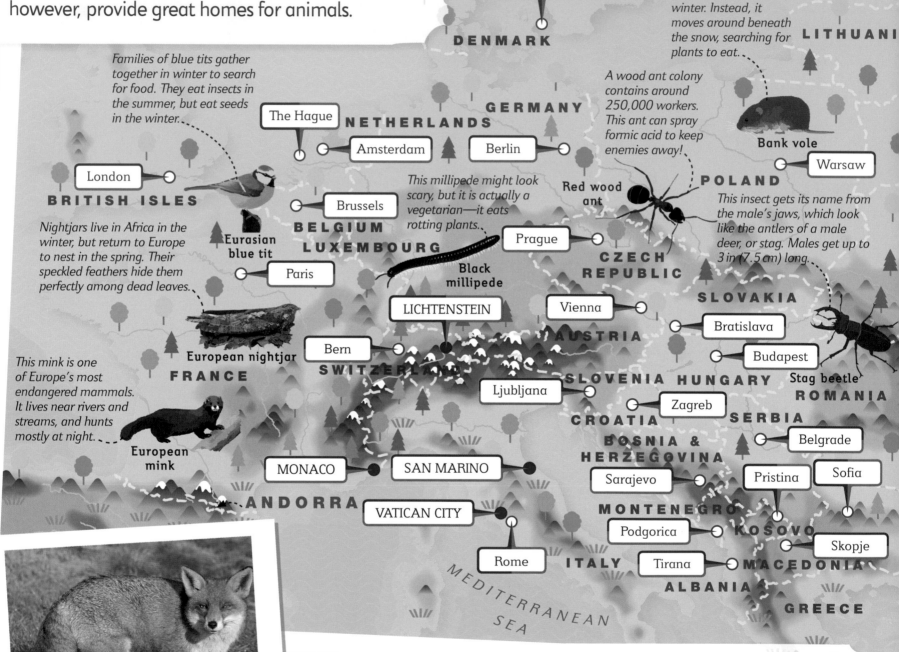

FINLAND

NORWAY

Oslo

Stockholm

BALTIC SEA

EST

SWEDEN

LATVIA

Copenhagen

This little rodent doesn't hibernate in winter. Instead, it moves around beneath the snow, searching for plants to eat.

LITHUANI

DENMARK

Families of blue tits gather together in winter to search for food. They eat insects in the summer, but eat seeds in the winter.

GERMANY

A wood ant colony contains around 250,000 workers. This ant can spray formic acid to keep enemies away!

The Hague

NETHERLANDS

Amsterdam

Berlin

Bank vole

London

Brussels

BELGIUM

Eurasian blue tit

BRITISH ISLES

Nightjars live in Africa in the winter, but return to Europe to nest in the spring. Their speckled feathers hide them perfectly among dead leaves.

Red wood ant

Warsaw

POLAND

This insect gets its name from the male's jaws, which look like the antlers of a male deer, or stag. Males get up to 3 in (7.5 cm) long.

This millipede might look scary, but it is actually a vegetarian—it eats rotting plants.

Prague

LUXEMBOURG

CZECH REPUBLIC

Paris

Black millipede

SLOVAKIA

European nightjar

LICHTENSTEIN

Vienna

Bratislava

Bern

AUSTRIA

Budapest

This mink is one of Europe's most endangered mammals. It lives near rivers and streams, and hunts mostly at night.

SWITZERLAND

SLOVENIA HUNGARY

Stag beetle

FRANCE

Ljubljana

ROMANIA

European mink

Zagreb

SERBIA

CROATIA

MONACO

SAN MARINO

BOSNIA & HERZEGOVINA

Belgrade

ANDORRA

VATICAN CITY

Sarajevo

Pristina

Sofia

MONTENEGRO

Podgorica

KOSOVO

Rome

ITALY

Tirana

Skopje

MACEDONIA

ALBANIA

MEDITERRANEAN SEA

GREECE

Red fox

This adaptable mammal can live almost anywhere—farms or city centers, marshes or mountaintops. It lives in more places in the world than any other carnivore.

52

A red fox's bushy tail is called a brush.

Location

There are areas of forest in mainland Europe from Portugal as far as Russia. Some get really hot in summer, while others are cool all year round.

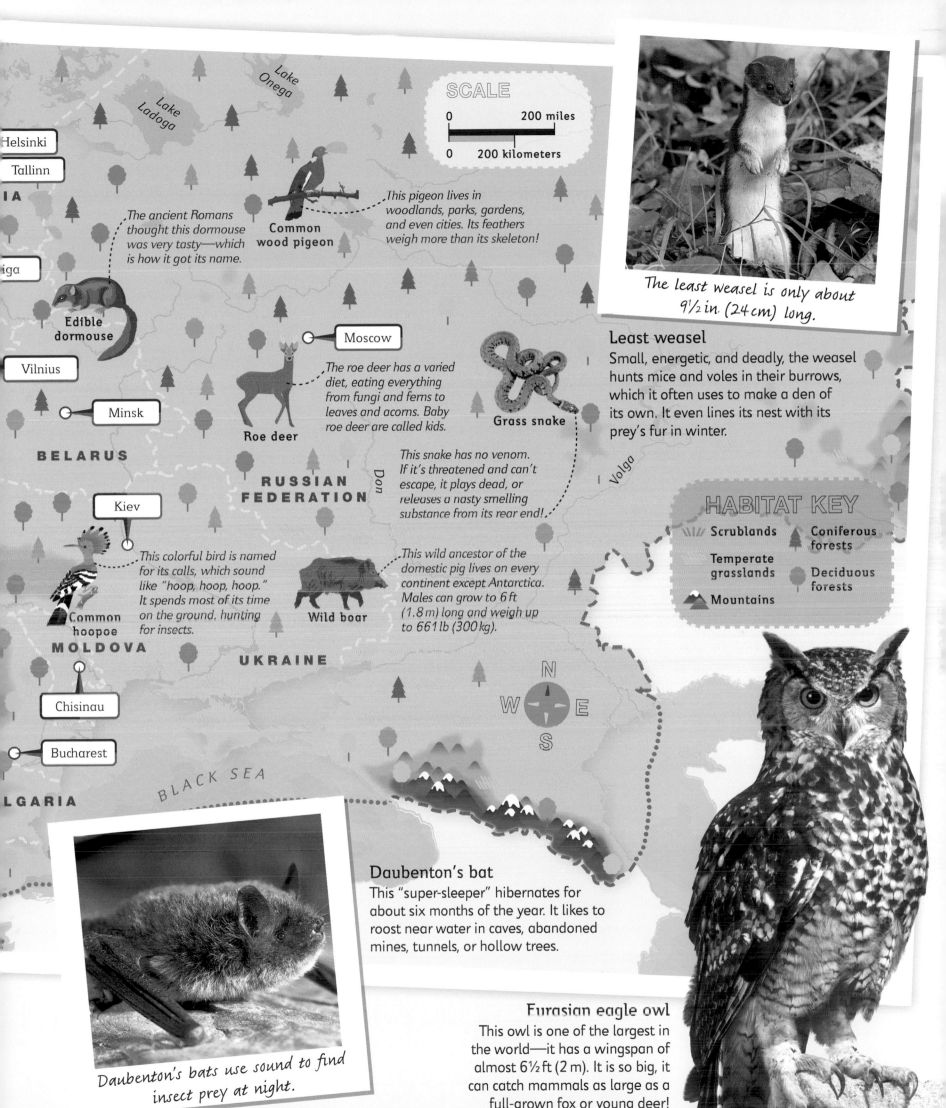

SCALE

0 — 200 miles

0 — 200 kilometers

Lake Ladoga

Lake Onega

Helsinki

Tallinn

...IA

...iga

Vilnius

Minsk

BELARUS

Kiev

MOLDOVA

Chisinau

Bucharest

...LGARIA

BLACK SEA

UKRAINE

RUSSIAN FEDERATION

Don

Volga

Moscow

The ancient Romans thought this dormouse was very tasty—which is how it got its name.

Edible dormouse

This pigeon lives in woodlands, parks, gardens, and even cities. Its feathers weigh more than its skeleton!

Common wood pigeon

The roe deer has a varied diet, eating everything from fungi and ferns to leaves and acorns. Baby roe deer are called kids.

Roe deer

Grass snake

This snake has no venom. If it's threatened and can't escape, it plays dead, or releases a nasty smelling substance from its rear end!

This colorful bird is named for its calls, which sound like "hoop, hoop, hoop." It spends most of its time on the ground, hunting for insects.

Common hoopoe

This wild ancestor of the domestic pig lives on every continent except Antarctica. Males can grow to 6 ft (1.8 m) long and weigh up to 661 lb (300 kg).

Wild boar

The least weasel is only about 9½ in. (24 cm) long.

Least weasel
Small, energetic, and deadly, the weasel hunts mice and voles in their burrows, which it often uses to make a den of its own. It even lines its nest with its prey's fur in winter.

HABITAT KEY

Scrublands
Temperate grasslands
Mountains
Coniferous forests
Deciduous forests

N W E S

Daubenton's bats use sound to find insect prey at night.

Daubenton's bat
This "super-sleeper" hibernates for about six months of the year. It likes to roost near water in caves, abandoned mines, tunnels, or hollow trees.

Eurasian eagle owl
This owl is one of the largest in the world—it has a wingspan of almost 6½ ft (2 m). It is so big, it can catch mammals as large as a full-grown fox or young deer!

The Alps

The mountains of the Alps divide the cooler northern parts of Europe from the warm southern parts. With mountain lakes, glaciers, meadows, and forests, there are plenty of places for different animals to live. As many as 30,000 different species make their home here.

Location
The Alps stretch through eight countries in total. The highest parts are always snowy, but in summer lower parts can reach 86°F (30°C).

GERMANY

AUSTRIA

SWITZERLAND

FRANCE

SLOVENIA

CROATIA

ITALY

LICHTENSTEIN

Bern

Ljubljana

This hoofed mammal is able to run up to 31 mph (50 kph), even on a snow-covered mountain!

Young shrews "caravan" behind their mother, by following each other in a line, holding onto the shrew in front by their mouth!

Alpine shrew

Chamois

Rock ptarmigan

This ptarmigan turns white in the winter to hide from predators in the snow.

Alpine chough

The endangered Apollo butterfly's bright-red wing spots fade in the sun, so older butterflies have spots that are more orange.

Apollo butterfly

The alpine chough has been seen soaring as high as 26,250 ft (8,000 m) above sea level!

Alpine ibex

The sure-footed ibex has long curved horns that grow up to 40 in (100 cm) long in males.

Alpine salamander

Although it mostly comes out at night, this little black salamander also ventures out in the daytime after rain.

HABITAT KEY

Scrublands

Mountains

Coniferous forests

Deciduous forests

SCALE

0 ——— 100 miles

0 ——— 100 kilometers

Pine marten
Powerful forelimbs and strong claws make martens excellent climbers. They even race through the trees to hunt squirrels.

Alpine marmot
The alpine marmot digs long, deep burrows where it hibernates for up to nine months of the year. When hibernating, a marmot breathes just one to two times a minute!

The marmot lives in high alpine meadows and pastures.

54

European steppe

The steppe is a temperate grassland habitat. Many animals here are seasonal visitors from other habitats, while some, such as hamsters and moles, live here all year round.

Black-bellied hamster

This hamster digs summer and fall burrows 19½ in (50 cm) below the ground's surface. Its winter burrow can be 6½ ft (2 m) deep. When swimming, this hamster inflates its cheek pouches to act like water wings!

Black fur on its underside gives the black-bellied hamster its name.

RUSSIAN FEDERATION

This big bird of prey can live for up to 32 years. It makes a nest, called an aerie, in a tall tree or on a cliff ledge.

Golden eagle

SCALE

0 — 200 miles

0 — 200 kilometers

Minsk

This pink and black starling eats locusts and other grasshoppers it finds on the steppe.

The colorful marbled polecat travels up to 0.6 miles (1 km) a night searching for food.

BELARUS

The mole's big forepaws are always turned outward to help it dig its underground tunnels.

Kiev   **Rosy starling**

UKRAINE

Although they each have their own burrow, there might be 6,000 giant mole rats in just 0.4 sq miles (1 sq km) of grassland!

Marbled polecat

HABITAT KEY

Temperate grasslands   Coniferous forests

Scrublands   Deciduous forests

Mountains

European mole   **Great bustard**   **Eurasian harvest mouse**
Weighing just 0.2 oz (6 g), the tiny harvest mouse is Europe's smallest rodent.

Giant mole rat

ROMANIA

This is the heaviest flying bird on Earth. Males weigh up to 35 lb (16 kg)!

Bucharest

BULGARIA

Sofia

MACEDONIA

N W E S

Location

The European steppe stretches from Romania in the west to the Ural Mountains in the east, where it merges with the Asian steppe.

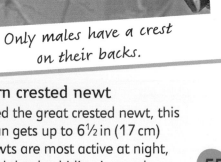

Only males have a crest on their backs.

Common nightingale

This little bird is plain to look at, but its song sets it apart. Nightingale songs are made up of an amazing variety of musical phrases and notes that other birds can't make.

Northern crested newt

Also called the great crested newt, this amphibian gets up to 6½ in (17 cm) long. Newts are most active at night, and spend the day hiding in ponds, or under damp logs or rocks.

Mediterranean scrubland

The coastal areas around the Mediterranean Sea contain rocky hills and flat, shrub-filled plains. This rare habitat is found in only a few places on Earth. Plants here can survive wildfires, and animals have to deal with hot, dry weather.

Mediterranean chameleon
This is one of only two chameleon species found in Europe. Its tongue is sticky to catch passing insects. It is also twice the length of its body!

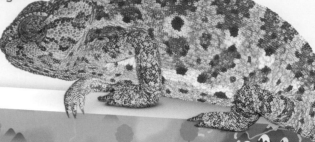

This wolf is thinner and smaller than other European wolves. It hunts rabbits, deer, wild boar, birds, and fish.

FRANCE

N W E S

Garonne

Rhône

MONACO

Mediterranean banded centipede

This centipede paralyzes its prey with a venomous bite and will give a human a painful nip too—so stay well away!

Ebro

PYRENEES

ANDORRA

Mediterranean tree frog

This frog is usually bright green or blue. It has suckers on its fingers and toes that let it climb with ease.

SPAIN

Iberian wolf

PORTUGAL

Madrid

Tagus

Jeweled lizard

Majorca

Sardinia   Corsica

The cuckoo lays its eggs in other birds' nests. When the cuckoo chick hatches, it pushes all the other eggs out—so the parent birds feed it instead!

Common cuckoo

Lisbon

This monkey is found in Africa and on the island of Gibraltar, near Spain. It is the only wild monkey in Europe.

Iberian ibex

The sapphire-like blue spots on its body give this lizard its name. It is the largest lizard in Europe at about 23½ in (60 cm) long.

Iberian pig

This pig is a farmed animal, but lives in open country, looking for mushrooms, roots, and acorns from cork oaks.

Barbary macaque

A type of wild goat, male Iberian ibexes have horns that grow up to 29½ in (75 cm) long!

MEDITERRANEAN SEA

SCALE

0   200 miles

0   200 kilometers

HABITAT KEY
- Scrublands
- Coniferous forests
- Wetlands
- Mountains
- Deciduous forests

European rabbit
The European rabbit is the ancestor of all pet rabbits in the world. Unlike its enemy, the Iberian lynx, the rabbit has been seen in yards and parks, and even in busy cities.

Location
This region includes the southern parts of Europe around the Mediterranean Sea, as well as islands like Crete that share a similar habitat.

Hummingbird hawk moth

This insect beats its wings so fast that they make a humming sound—just like the birds it's named after. It feeds on nectar made by flowers like buddleia and honeysuckle.

The hawk moth will return to a nectar-rich flower day after day.

Iberian lynx

Fewer than 900 adult Iberian lynxes are left in the wild, making it one of the most endangered cats on Earth—but the good news is this figure is more than twice the number of wild lynxes alive a few years ago!

The Iberian lynx mostly hunts just one animal—the European rabbit.

Zagreb

CROATIA

Golden jackal

SAN MARINO

BOSNIA & HERZEGOVINA

Belgrade

ROMANIA

The golden jackal is found in many places, including southeastern Europe, northern Africa, and southern Asia.

ITALY

Sarajevo

SERBIA

Rome

VATICAN CITY

MONTENEGRO

Pristina

The cork oak is one of few trees that can grow new bark. The cork bark is harvested once every nine years to make bottle stoppers and other items.

ADRIATIC SEA

Podgorica

KOSOVO

BULGARIA

Cork oak

Tirana

Skopje

MACEDONIA

The magpie is so smart that it can make and use tools. It eats insects and seeds, and will even steal other birds' eggs.

ALBANIA

Dalmatian pelican

GREECE

In addition to making other sounds, this pelican barks and hisses! To feed, it fills up its beak pouch with water and fish. It then drains the water so it can swallow the fish.

Eurasian magpie

Marginated tortoise

This plant-eating tortoise lives mostly in Greece, in thorny, rocky, scrubby areas.

Sicily

Athens

MEDITERRANEAN SEA

MALTA

Crete

Mediterranean house gecko

This little gecko is about 4 in (10 cm) long and weighs about as much as a sugar cube. It is also called a "moon lizard" because it mostly comes out at night. It eats small cockroaches and moths.

Białowieża Forest

Białowieża is lowland Europe's only old-growth, or "primeval," forest. Forests like this once covered all of northeastern Europe. Its many different trees and habitats mean Białowieża is home to thousands of animals, including the rare European bison!

Red deer Red deer find leaves, small twigs, and bark to eat in the fall and winter, and herbs and grasses during the summer.

Pine marten Pine martens are related to weasels but, unlike weasels, they hunt in the trees. They chase small mammals such as squirrels.

All domestic dogs are descended from the gray wolf.

Gray wolf

The gray wolf is found in Europe, North America, and Asia. Packs of four to five wolves hunt deer, elk, wild boar, rabbits, and beavers.

Red fox Foxes feed on a wide variety of foods. In Białowieża, they eat yellow-necked mice, hares, and the carcasses of red deer killed by wolves or lynxes.

Common toad

Many parts of this forest are wet, including rare places known as "spruce bog forests," where coniferous spruce trees grow in very wet ground. These habitats make a perfect home for the common toad!

A male and female red fox have a territory that they share, which is where they raise their young.

Old-growth forests have plenty of standing dead trees as well as live ones. Woodpecker nests or holes where the tree has rotted make ideal bat roosts.

Great spotted woodpecker
Woodpeckers nest in holes made in tree trunks. They search for tasty insect prey in the bark.

European bison The bison is Europe's largest land mammal. There are around 900 in Białowieża forest.

Tawny owl This woodland owl hunts at night for birds, rodents, amphibians such as frogs, and bats to eat.

Noctule bat
Noctule bats nest in hollow trees. The holes must be high enough to avoid predators such as pine martens. Noctules are one of the first bats to come out at night, and hunt moths and flying ants.

Eurasian red squirrel
Eurasian red squirrels like to eat seeds, especially from conifer trees.

Yellow-necked mouse
This mouse prefers living in woodland, because it eats a lot of tree seeds. It is also an excellent tree climber!

Eurasian badger Badgers are common in forests. In addition to plenty of worms to eat, they find lots of hollow trees, which they use as daytime shelters

Location
Białowieża Forest covers 579 sq miles (1,500 sq km) across Poland and Belarus. Temperatures range from 21°F (-6°C) in winter to 75°F (24°C) in summer.

Eurasian beaver
The Eurasian beaver disappeared from Białowieża in the mid-19th century due to hunting. It was reintroduced in 1956. Today, they live all along the rivers, streams, and ponds throughout the forest.

Beavers produce an oily substance that keeps their fur waterproof.

59

Asia

Welcome to Earth's largest continent! Asia contains half the world's human population, but there is still a lot of land for wildlife. Habitats here include vast deserts, grassy plains, snowy mountains, and dense, green rain forests.

Savanna

This region in northern India is warm all year round. It has the tallest grasslands in the world—some grow more than 10ft (3 m) high! The grasslands provide food for deer and rhinos, and cover for predators such as the tiger.

City wildlife

The Turkish city of Istanbul is rich in wildlife—337 of the country's 483 bird species, such as this seagull, live here. The city is also part of an important migration route for hundreds of thousands of storks, raptors, and water birds each year.

MEDITERRANEAN SEA

BLACK SEA

TURKEY

CYPRUS

GEORGIA

ARMENIA

AZERBAIJAN

LEBANON

SYRIA

ISRAEL

JORDAN

IRAQ

KUWAIT

CASPIAN SEA

IRAN

TURKMENISTAN

UZBEKISTAN

KYRGYZSTAN

TAJIKISTAN

AFGHANISTAN

KAZAKHSTAN

RED SEA

SAUDI ARABIA

BAHRAIN

QATAR

UNITED ARAB EMIRATES

YEMEN

OMAN

PAKISTAN

NEPAL

INDIA

GULF OF ADEN

ARABIAN SEA

Socotra

BAY OF

SRI LANKA

N W E S

Maldives

INDIAN

Arabian highlands

The Arabian highlands are made of the mountains and high plateaus that border the desert of the Arabian Peninsula, in southwest Asia. The highlands are cooler than the desert, and have more rainfall, so shrubs and grasses can grow. These plants are food for animals such as camels.

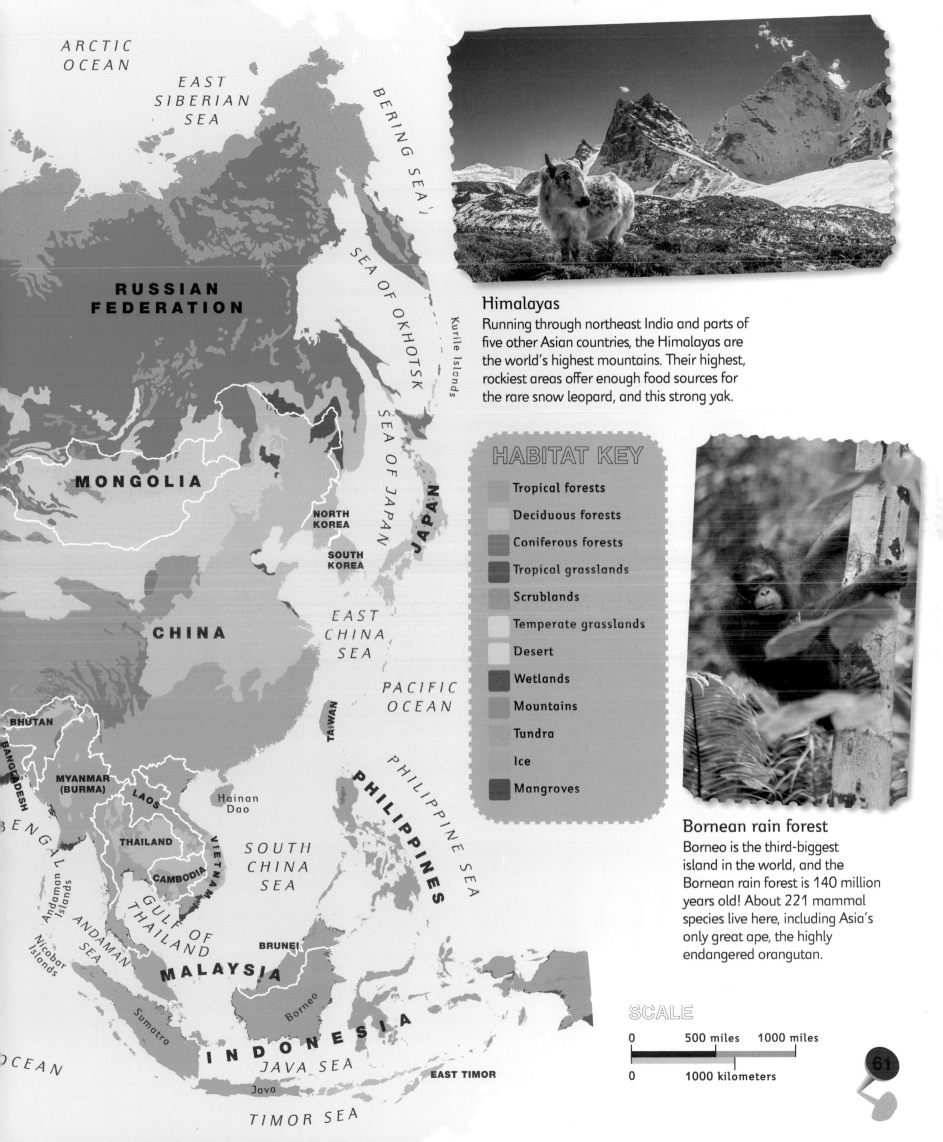

ARCTIC
OCEAN

EAST
SIBERIAN
SEA

BERING SEA

RUSSIAN
FEDERATION

SEA OF OKHOTSK

Kurile Islands

MONGOLIA

NORTH
KOREA

SEA OF JAPAN

JAPAN

SOUTH
KOREA

CHINA

EAST
CHINA
SEA

PACIFIC
OCEAN

TAIWAN

PHILIPPINE SEA

PHILIPPINES

BHUTAN

BANGLADESH

MYANMAR
(BURMA)

LAOS

Hainan
Dao

BENGAL

THAILAND

CAMBODIA

VIETNAM

SOUTH
CHINA
SEA

Andaman
Islands

ANDAMAN
SEA

GULF OF
THAILAND

Nicobar
Islands

BRUNEI

MALAYSIA

Sumatra

Borneo

OCEAN

INDONESIA

JAVA SEA

EAST TIMOR

Java

TIMOR SEA

Himalayas

Running through northeast India and parts of five other Asian countries, the Himalayas are the world's highest mountains. Their highest, rockiest areas offer enough food sources for the rare snow leopard, and this strong yak.

HABITAT KEY

Tropical forests

Deciduous forests

Coniferous forests

Tropical grasslands

Scrublands

Temperate grasslands

Desert

Wetlands

Mountains

Tundra

Ice

Mangroves

Bornean rain forest

Borneo is the third-biggest island in the world, and the Bornean rain forest is 140 million years old! About 221 mammal species live here, including Asia's only great ape, the highly endangered orangutan.

SCALE

| 0 | 500 miles | 1000 miles |

| 0 | 1000 kilometers |

Russian taiga

Taiga is also called "snow forest." It's found in cool, high places, like in northeast Russia, and is made up of coniferous forests. Animals use trees for food and shelter, and as places to hide from predators.

KARA SEA

Fur-covered flaps of skin linking its legs let this tiny squirrel glide from tree to tree.

Siberian flying squirrel

Brown bear
The most widespread of all bear species, the brown bear eats mostly roots, berries, and other parts of plants, but it will also hunt animals. Adults can be more than 7 ft (2 m) tall when they stand on their hind legs.

The sable is a member of the weasel family. It hunts chipmunks, mice, and birds.

Sable

A brown bear takes to the river to hunt for salmon.

This deer has fangs! They're really tusklike teeth that the males use to fight each other.

Ob

Irtysh

Yenisei

Siberian musk deer

Fast-growing birch trees shed their bark like tissue paper as they grow.

This wapiti is a large type of deer that forms herds of 100 or more in the fall.

Silver birch

The saiga's swollen, flexible nose hangs over its mouth, helping keep out the dust kicked up by its herd in summer.

Siberian wapiti

Saiga antelope

Siberian tiger
This is the world's biggest wild cat. Males weigh up to 660 lb (300 kg). It even has a mane, like a lion's, to help keep its neck warm in cold Siberian winters.

HABITAT KEY
- Wetlands
- Mountains
- Snow and ice
- Coniferous forests
- Deciduous forests

62

Ural owl
This big owl hunts rodents, frogs, and birds that it spots from its perch. In spring, it sings a courtship duet with its lifelong mate.

The Ural owl aggressively defends its territory, chasing away intruders.

This is the only chipmunk found outside North America. It has five dark and four white stripes running along its back.

Siberian chipmunk

Both male and female snow sheep have big, curved horns that grow in a corkscrew shape as they get older.

Snow sheep

Its main home is the taiga, but this little bird is sometimes spotted in Scotland and North America.

Siberian rubythroat

Lena

Blue robins often look for food near rivers, but they never stray far from the forest.

N
W · E
S

SCALE

0 ——————— 300 miles

0 ——————— 300 kilometers

Siberian blue robin

This seal lives only in Lake Baikal, which is an icy, freshwater lake in Russian Siberia.

Baikal seal

Lake Baikal

Wood frogs spend the winter hibernating in holes on river bottoms.

Siberian wood frog

Location
Taiga stretches over northeast Russia, eastward to the Pacific Ocean. Summers are short, but the winters are long and snowy.

Black woodpecker
Strong neck muscles and a sharp bill make this bird a champion wood borer. It chisels out holes in tree trunks, where it lays its eggs.

Asian steppe

A steppe is a high, grassy, mostly treeless plain. Animals here live on grass and other plants— or on the animals that do! They must be able to survive freezing winters, hot summers, and harsh winds, and to go long periods without water. On the steppe, water is in short supply.

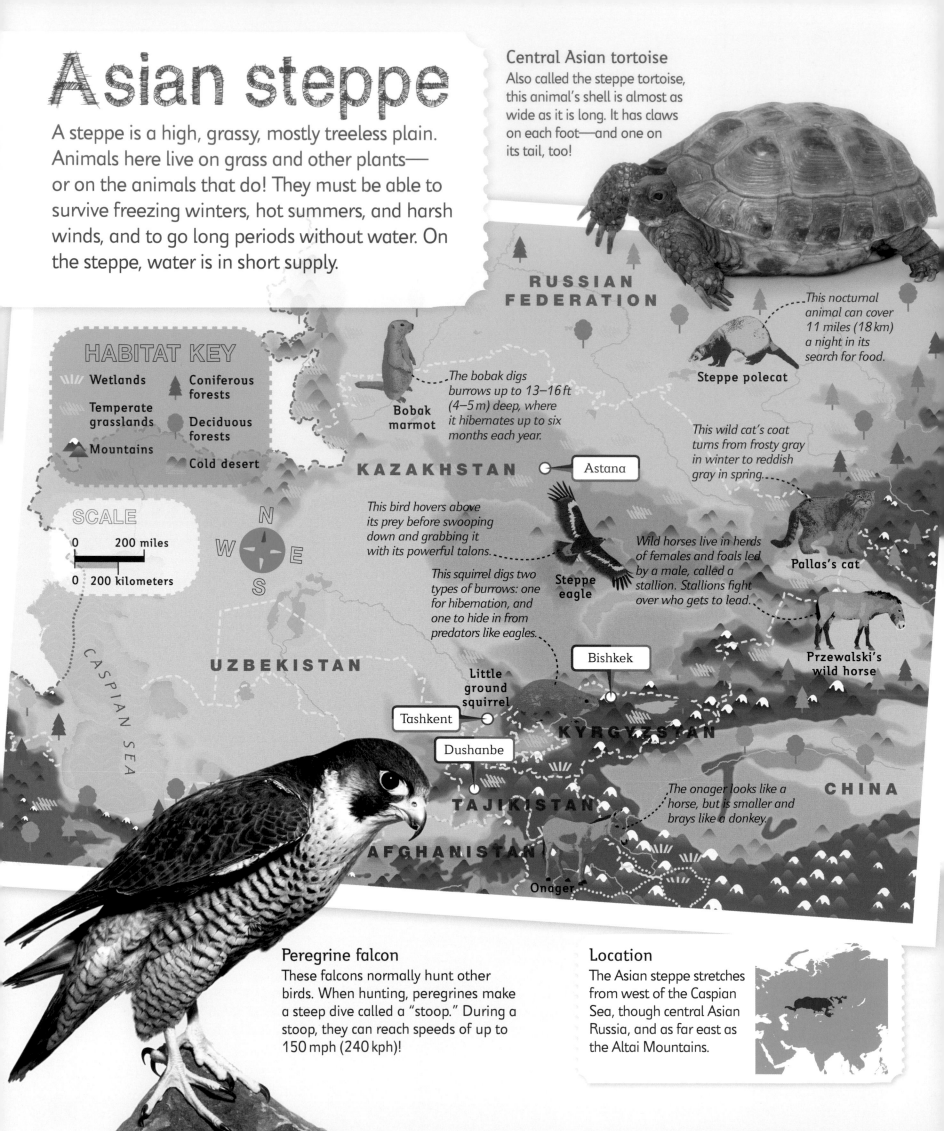

Central Asian tortoise
Also called the steppe tortoise, this animal's shell is almost as wide as it is long. It has claws on each foot—and one on its tail, too!

RUSSIAN FEDERATION

This nocturnal animal can cover 11 miles (18 km) a night in its search for food.

Steppe polecat

HABITAT KEY

- 〰 Wetlands
- 🌲 Coniferous forests
- 〰 Temperate grasslands
- ⬤ Deciduous forests
- ⛰ Mountains
- Cold desert

The bobak digs burrows up to 13–16 ft (4–5 m) deep, where it hibernates up to six months each year.

Bobak marmot

This wild cat's coat turns from frosty gray in winter to reddish gray in spring.

KAZAKHSTAN — Astana

This bird hovers above its prey before swooping down and grabbing it with its powerful talons.

Steppe eagle

Pallas's cat

SCALE

0 ___ 200 miles

0 ___ 200 kilometers

This squirrel digs two types of burrows: one for hibernation, and one to hide in from predators like eagles.

Wild horses live in herds of females and foals led by a male, called a stallion. Stallions fight over who gets to lead.

Przewalski's wild horse

UZBEKISTAN

Little ground squirrel

Bishkek

Tashkent

KYRGYZSTAN

Dushanbe

CHINA

The onager looks like a horse, but is smaller and brays like a donkey.

TAJIKISTAN

AFGHANISTAN

Onager

Peregrine falcon
These falcons normally hunt other birds. When hunting, peregrines make a steep dive called a "stoop." During a stoop, they can reach speeds of up to 150 mph (240 kph)!

Location
The Asian steppe stretches from west of the Caspian Sea, though central Asian Russia, and as far east as the Altai Mountains.

CASPIAN SEA

A secret toadhead agama stands alert.

Secret toadhead agama

The insect-eating agama keeps several secrets. It may look like a regular desert lizard, but when it displays, it opens its mouth to reveal a deep reddish pink and expands two spiny cheek flaps.

Location

There are deserts in Kazakhstan, Uzbekistan, and Turkmenistan, and parts of Afghanistan, Pakistan, and Iran.

When a predator is near, this hedgehog growls and hisses like a cat, then rolls itself into a protective ball.

Astana

The corsac fox uses its long, wide ears to listen for rodent noises in the desert.

Long-eared hedgehog

KAZAKHSTAN

Corsac fox

SCALE

0   200 miles

0   200 kilometers

N W E S

At up to 13 in (33 cm) long, this is the largest gerbil on Earth.

Bishkek

This is the world's most venomous true cobra. Though it lives in the desert, it is very good at swimming.

UZBEKISTAN

Tashkent

KYRGYZSTAN

Great gerbil

This hare comes out at night to feed on desert plants. It rests in a shallow scrape in the ground during the day.

Central Asian cobra

Yerevan

CHINA

AZERBAIJAN

TURKMENISTAN

Dushanbe

TAJIKISTAN

ARMENIA

The wild goat lives in dry, rocky areas. Its curved horns have a very sharp inside edge.

Baku

Ashgabat

Tolai hare

Tehran

Kabul

Tehran

Wild goat

Islamabad

Baghdad

IRAN

AFGHANISTAN

PAKISTAN

Central Asian deserts

There are different kinds of deserts here. Some are salty and sandy. Others are rocky or have clay soil. All are dry. Water is found mostly near desert borders where rivers can overflow.

Goitered gazelle

A big, swollen tube on its throat gives this gazelle its name. It also gives males an extra-loud voice.

HABITAT KEY

- Wetlands
- Temperate grasslands
- Mountains
- Cold desert
- Hot desert
- Coniferous forests
- Deciduous forests
- Tropical forests

Tibetan Plateau

This high, flat region of Asia is surrounded by mountains. It's so high that it's often called the "roof of the world." The animals that live here have to deal with thin air and bitter winters.

HABITAT KEY
- Tropical forests
- Coniferous forests
- Tropical grasslands
- Deciduous forests
- Mountains
- Cold desert

Many kinds of plants grow on the plateau, including this serratula, a type of thistle.

Himalayan alpine serratula

Location
This region includes Tibet and parts of southwest China. Summers are dry and warm, and winters are often below freezing.

Islamabad

This little relative of the rabbit is so suited to rocky ground that it often nests in a pile of stones!

Himalayan mouse hare

This large, cowlike animal has extra-big lungs that help it to get enough oxygen from the thin air.

Wild yak

Asiatic black bear
This bear is also called the "moon bear" due to the pale, crescent-shaped band on its chest. It spends about half of its life up in trees.

PAKISTAN

The tahr is a wild goat that has hooves with rubberlike cores. These help it grip onto smooth rocks.

Himalayan tahr

NEPAL

HIMALAYAS

New Delhi

INDIA

N W E S

Himalayan wolf

Kathmandu

The Himalayan wolf is a rare type of gray wolf. Some are almost white—like snow on the Himalayas!

Himalayan marmots dig very deep burrows to hibernate in.

Himalayan marmot
Nicknamed the "Tibetan snow pig," this ground squirrel is one of the only mammals on Earth that lives above 16,400 ft (5,000 m).

When threatened, the mountain weasel scares away predators with a foul-smelling spray called musk.

Mountain weasel

Pandas are the only bears that eat just plants.

ALTUN MOUNTAINS

CHINA

This bird picks up bones in its claws and carries them high into the air. It then drops the bones on rocks to shatter them into bite-sized pieces.

Bearded vulture

Giant panda
The giant panda lives in six forests in central China. It spends 10 to 16 hours a day eating mostly bamboo, and sleeps the rest of the time.

The chiru is a type of antelope. It has soft wool, called shahtoosh, which is very good at keeping it warm through winter.

Chiru

Also called the Himalayan blue sheep, the bharal has a bluish sheen to its gray coat. This makes it hard for its enemies to see it against rocky cliffs.

This very rare fox hunts rodents and lizards. Its slitlike eyes help to lessen glare from the sun.

Bharal

Kiang

Herds of kiang can have as many as 400 animals. When they travel, kiangs follow their female leader in single file.

Tibetan sand fox

This raccoonlike animal is also called the "fire fox" or "fire cat" due to its striking red fur.

Thimphu

Tibetan toad

Red panda

BHUTAN

This toad is one of the very few amphibians that are able to live so high up.

MYANMAR

BANGLADESH

Snow leopard
These cats have a thick, spotted coat that keeps them warm and helps them blend in when hunting. They keep their face warm when they sleep by covering it with their furry tail.

East Asian forests

Eastern Asia's deciduous forests are full of trees like oak and ash, as well as some walnut and birch. With streams and rivers, mountains and grassland edges, they are a haven for animals.

Ulan Bator

YABLONOI MOUNTAINS

MONGOLIA

Chinese peacock butterfly
This forest butterfly's size depends on what time of the year it comes out of its cocoon. Spring Chinese peacocks have a wingspan of up to 3 in (8 cm). Summer ones have a wingspan up to 5 in (12 cm).

A Chinese peacock butterfly feeds on a spider lily plant.

Japanese sika deer
The sika is a small deer—males are only 3 ft (95 cm) at shoulder height. They make strange noises, too, such as the male's long, whistlelike call that sounds like a siren.

Beijing

This snake eats poisonous toads, absorbs the poisons, then releases them later from its neck glands!

Asian tiger keelback

This monkey has a blue face! It spends 95 percent of its time in the trees.

Golden snub-nosed monkey

Huang He

Male Baikal teals make a deep chuckling sound—wot-wot-wot!

Baikal teal

Earth's largest amphibian grows to 6 ft (1.8 m) long. That's longer than many adult humans are tall!

Yangtze

CHINA

Chinese giant salamander

This is the smallest of the "big cats." Cloudlike spots help this leopard blend in with its forest home.

Clouded leopard

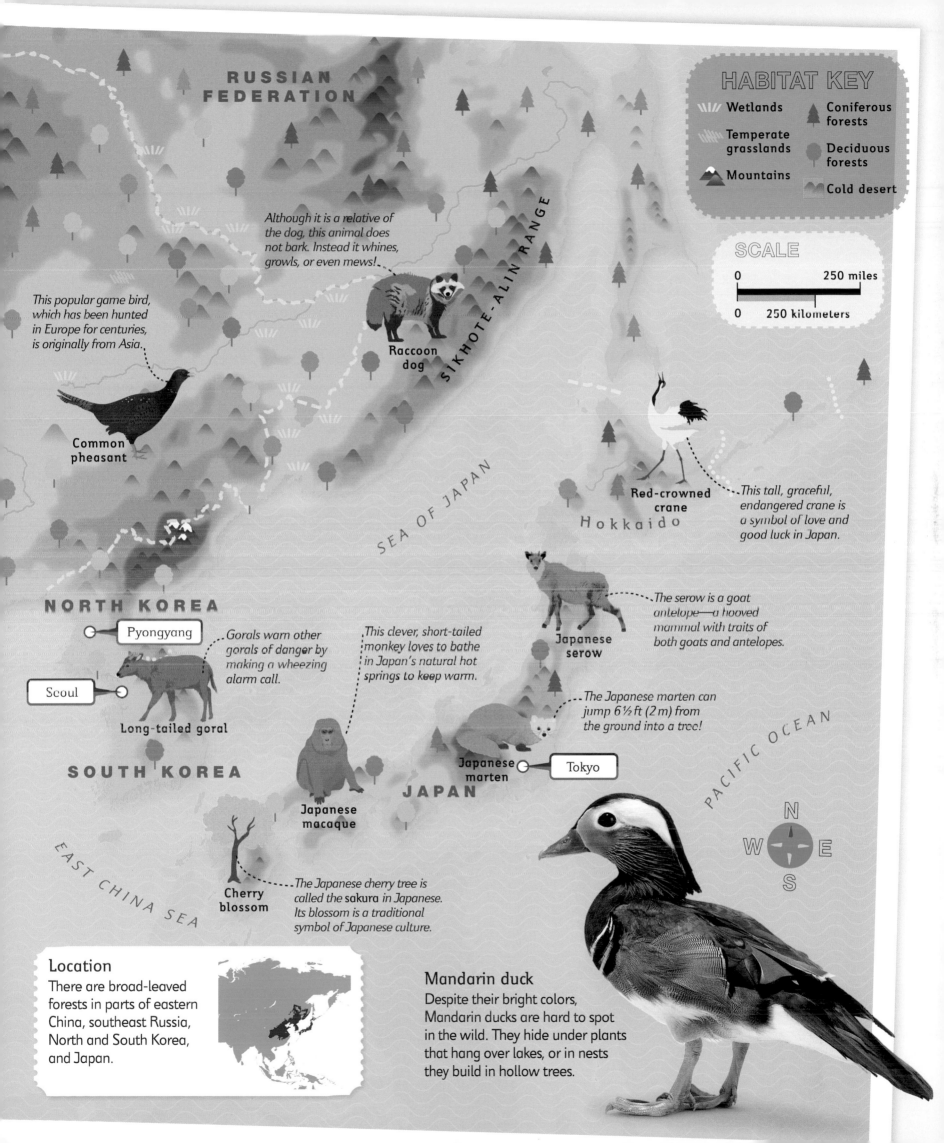

RUSSIAN FEDERATION

Although it is a relative of the dog, this animal does not bark. Instead it whines, growls, or even mews!

SIKHOTE-ALIN RANGE

Raccoon dog

This popular game bird, which has been hunted in Europe for centuries, is originally from Asia.

Common pheasant

Red-crowned crane

This tall, graceful, endangered crane is a symbol of love and good luck in Japan.

Hokkaido

SEA OF JAPAN

NORTH KOREA

○ Pyongyang

Gorals warn other gorals of danger by making a wheezing alarm call.

This clever, short-tailed monkey loves to bathe in Japan's natural hot springs to keep warm.

Japanese serow

The serow is a goat antelope—a hooved mammal with traits of both goats and antelopes.

Scoul ○

Long-tailed goral

The Japanese marten can jump 6½ ft (2 m) from the ground into a tree!

SOUTH KOREA

Japanese marten ○ Tokyo

JAPAN

Japanese macaque

PACIFIC OCEAN

N
W ⊕ E
S

EAST CHINA SEA

Cherry blossom

The Japanese cherry tree is called the sakura in Japanese. Its blossom is a traditional symbol of Japanese culture.

Location

There are broad-leaved forests in parts of eastern China, southeast Russia, North and South Korea, and Japan.

Mandarin duck

Despite their bright colors, Mandarin ducks are hard to spot in the wild. They hide under plants that hang over lakes, or in nests they build in hollow trees.

Arabian Peninsula

The Arabian Peninsula is a hot, dry part of the world, and it is covered by sandy deserts. The animals that live here have special ways of dealing with its harsh conditions.

Arabian partridge
This partridge lives on the ground, where it looks for seeds, grass, and insects to eat. The female lays her eggs in a shallow, scooped-out hole.

Partridges run rather than fly away when threatened.

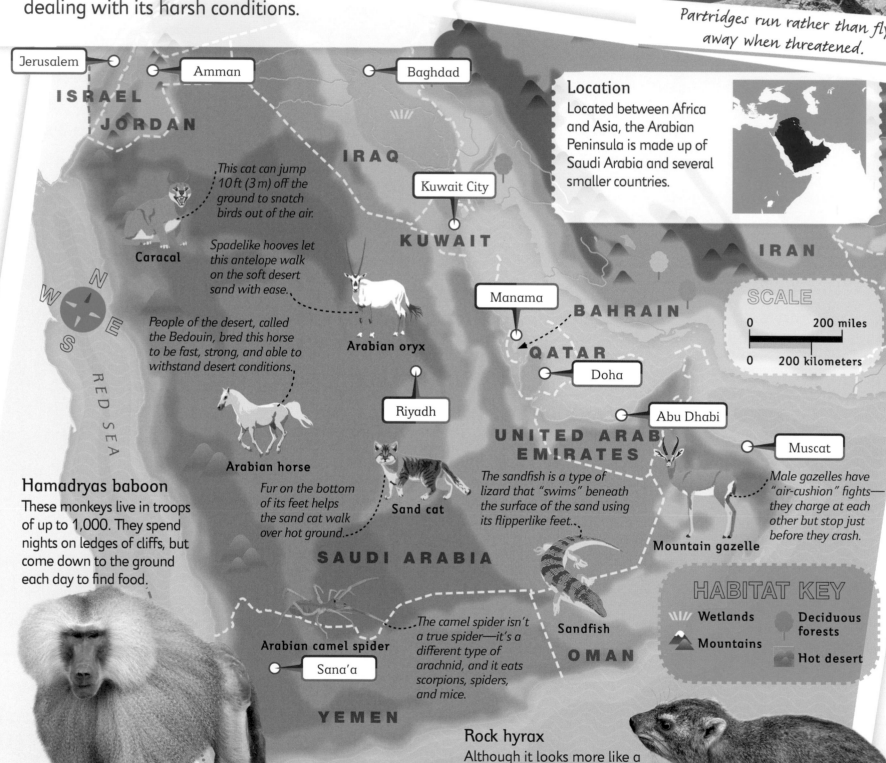

Jerusalem

Amman

Baghdad

ISRAEL

JORDAN

IRAQ

Kuwait City

KUWAIT

IRAN

Location
Located between Africa and Asia, the Arabian Peninsula is made up of Saudi Arabia and several smaller countries.

This cat can jump 10 ft (3 m) off the ground to snatch birds out of the air.

Caracal

Spadelike hooves let this antelope walk on the soft desert sand with ease.

Manama

BAHRAIN

SCALE

| 0 | 200 miles |
| 0 | 200 kilometers |

Arabian oryx

People of the desert, called the Bedouin, bred this horse to be fast, strong, and able to withstand desert conditions.

QATAR

Doha

Riyadh

Abu Dhabi

UNITED ARAB EMIRATES

Muscat

Arabian horse

Hamadryas baboon
These monkeys live in troops of up to 1,000. They spend nights on ledges of cliffs, but come down to the ground each day to find food.

Fur on the bottom of its feet helps the sand cat walk over hot ground.

Sand cat

The sandfish is a type of lizard that "swims" beneath the surface of the sand using its flipperlike feet.

Male gazelles have "air-cushion" fights— they charge at each other but stop just before they crash.

Mountain gazelle

SAUDI ARABIA

HABITAT KEY
- \\|// Wetlands
- ⛰ Mountains
- ● Deciduous forests
- ▰ Hot desert

Arabian camel spider

Sana'a

The camel spider isn't a true spider—it's a different type of arachnid, and it eats scorpions, spiders, and mice.

Sandfish

OMAN

YEMEN

Rock hyrax
Although it looks more like a guinea pig, the plant-eating rock hyrax is related to the elephant. It even grows two tiny tusks!

India's forests can be wet or dry, but all are warm and tropical. Many trees have broad leaves that they lose in the dry season. For animals, the forests provide food and shelter. However, since trees are cut down for wood or to make farmland, animals like the Bengal tiger have fewer places to live.

Location

Indian forests stretch from the Himalayan mountains south to the Indian Ocean. The weather here is hot or warm most of the year.

PAKISTAN

INDIA

Ganges

Yamuna

New Delhi

Bengal tiger
This tiger's canine teeth (fangs) grow up to 4 in (10 cm) long.

Male peafowl are called peacocks. They use their bright, eyespotted feathers to attract mates.

Ganges

Indian peafowl

Indian grey mongoose
Mongooses kill scorpions by throwing them against a hard surface until they crack.

Narmada

The cobra hunts lizards, rodents, and frogs. Venom from its bite stops its prey from being able to move.

Indian cobra

Godavani

The Indian rhino's horn grows to 2 ft (60 cm) long. It's made from keratin—just like our hair.

Indian rhinoceros

Krishna

The giant squirrel builds nests in trees that are the same size as eagles' nests.

Indian giant squirrel

ARABIAN SEA

Asia's largest land mammal is much smaller than its African cousin. It spends three-quarters of its day eating plants.

Asian elephant

SCALE

0	200 miles

0	200 kilometers

HABITAT KEY

- Wetlands
- Mountains
- Cold desert
- Coniferous forests
- Deciduous forests
- Tropical forests

SRI LANKA

Colombo

Sri Jayawardenepura Kotte

BAY OF BENGAL

Andaman and Nicobar islands

The Indian giant hornet's bright orange color makes it easy to spot.

Indian giant hornet

The giant hornet is the world's largest—and probably angriest—wasp. It grows up to 2 in (5 cm) long and will sting anything that even slightly disturbs its nest.

Sloth bear

The shy sloth bear digs ants and termites with its long, curved claws. As it laps them up, its loud slurping can be heard from 590 ft (180 m) away.

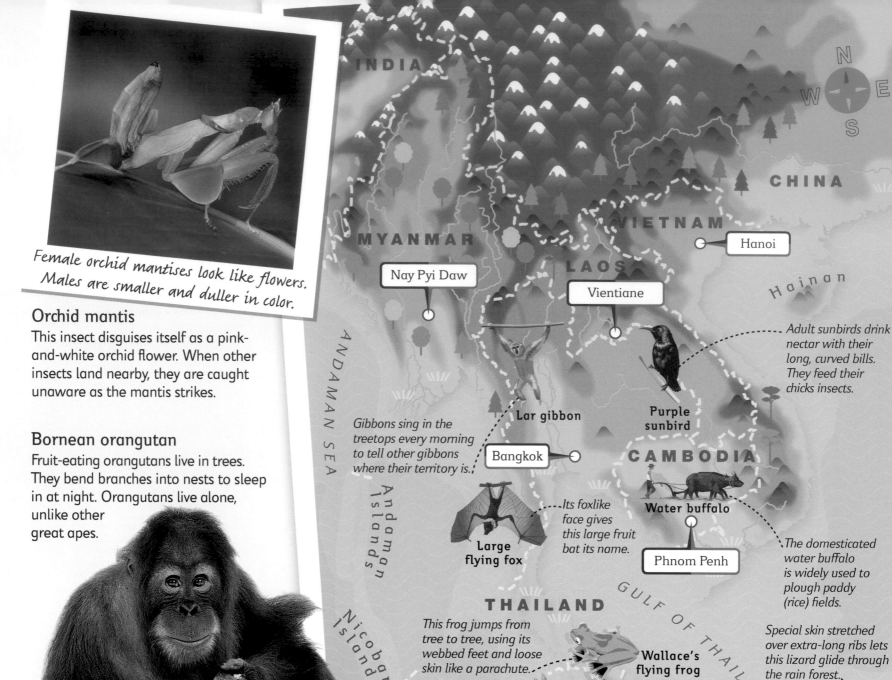

Female orchid mantises look like flowers. Males are smaller and duller in color.

Orchid mantis

This insect disguises itself as a pink-and-white orchid flower. When other insects land nearby, they are caught unaware as the mantis strikes.

Bornean orangutan

Fruit-eating orangutans live in trees. They bend branches into nests to sleep in at night. Orangutans live alone, unlike other great apes.

Southeast Asian rain forest

The Southeast Asian rain forests are some of the oldest on Earth, and they are home to hundreds of animal species. As the rain forests are cut down, however, amazing animals like the Sumatran rhinoceros become rarer and rarer.

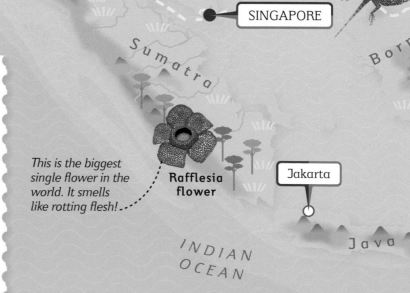

INDIA

CHINA

MYANMAR

VIETNAM

Nay Pyi Daw

Hanoi

LAOS

Hainan

Vientiane

Adult sunbirds drink nectar with their long, curved bills. They feed their chicks insects.

ANDAMAN SEA

Gibbons sing in the treetops every morning to tell other gibbons where their territory is.

Lar gibbon

Purple sunbird

Bangkok

CAMBODIA

Andaman Islands

Its foxlike face gives this large fruit bat its name.

Water buffalo

Large flying fox

Phnom Penh

The domesticated water buffalo is widely used to plough paddy (rice) fields.

THAILAND

GULF OF THAILAND

Nicobar Islands

This frog jumps from tree to tree, using its webbed feet and loose skin like a parachute.

Wallace's flying frog

Special skin stretched over extra-long ribs lets this lizard glide through the rain forest.

This rare, endangered rain-forest rhino has two horns.

Sumatran rhinoceros

Putrajaya

MALAYSIA

Kuala Lumpur

Common flying dragon

SINGAPORE

Sumatra

Borneo

This is the biggest single flower in the world. It smells like rotting flesh!

Rafflesia flower

Jakarta

INDIAN OCEAN

Java

Taipei

TAIWAN

Location
Lots of countries make up Southeast Asia, including many island nations. All are tropical, with a rainy monsoon season and a hot, dry season.

A big "sail" of skin on its tail helps drive the soa-soa water lizard forward when it swims.

HABITAT KEY
- Wetlands
- Mountains
- Tropical forests

Soa-soa water lizard

Manila

SCALE

0   200 miles

0   200 kilometers

One sting from a ribbontail stingray can kill a would-be predator.

Ribbontail stingray
This stingray swims in shallow water, looking for crabs, shrimp, and small fish to eat. Its bright-blue spots and stripes warn other sea creatures to stay away.

PHILIPPINES

PACIFIC OCEAN

SOUTH CHINA SEA

SULU SEA

Just 6 in (16 cm) tall, this little primate can turn its head right around to look backward!

Philippine tarsier

P a l a u

This species of humpback dolphin is usually gray, but it can also be white, or even pink!

Indo-Pacific humpback dolphin

King cobra
The king cobra can grow up to 18 ft (5.5 m) long. It lives almost entirely off other snakes, which it hunts by sight and smell. Unusually, this snake doesn't hiss—it growls!

BRUNEI

The world's smallest type of bear uses its long tongue to lap up insects, but its favorite food is fruit.

Sun bear

MOLUCCA SEA

North Maluku

New Guinea

Only male birds of paradise have amazing, colorful feathers, which they show off to attract females.

INDONESIA

Proboscis monkey

Sulawesi

M a l u k u

Male proboscis monkeys' huge noses help to make their calls louder.

The world's biggest lizard, the Komodo dragon grows up to 6 ft (2 m) long. Its venomous bite can kill a water buffalo!

Greater bird of paradise

JAVA SEA

EAST TIMOR

B a l i

Komodo dragon

Dili

Gobi desert

The Gobi is Asia's largest desert. It spans more than 460,000 sq miles (1.2 million sq km). Temperatures here can be as scorching hot as 122°F (50°C) and as freezing cold as -40°F (-40°C), but many tough animal species are able to survive despite the extreme conditions.

Gobi bear This is the Earth's rarest bear. Fewer than 50 Gobi bears remain in the desert, their only home.

Mongolian wild ass The wild ass waits for rare rain showers. After the showers, it can feed on fresh grass.

Dinosaur fossil
The Gobi tells us a lot about prehistoric wildlife. Hundreds of dinosaur fossils of many types have been found here—including some from 250 million years ago! This was also first place in the world where dinosaur eggs were identified.

Mongolian marmot This rodent spends winters in its burrow, where it is safe from predators such as eagles.

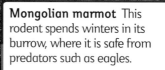

Long-eared jerboa This tiny, mouselike jerboa hops around the desert at night, looking for tasty insects to eat.

Marbled polecats are named after the pattern on their backs.

Marbled polecat
This little predator doesn't see very well, but it has no trouble finding most of its prey by smell. It hunts rodents, birds, and reptiles—mostly during cool desert nights.

This jerboa's enormous ears are almost as long as its body! Scientists think they release heat, keeping the jerboa cool.

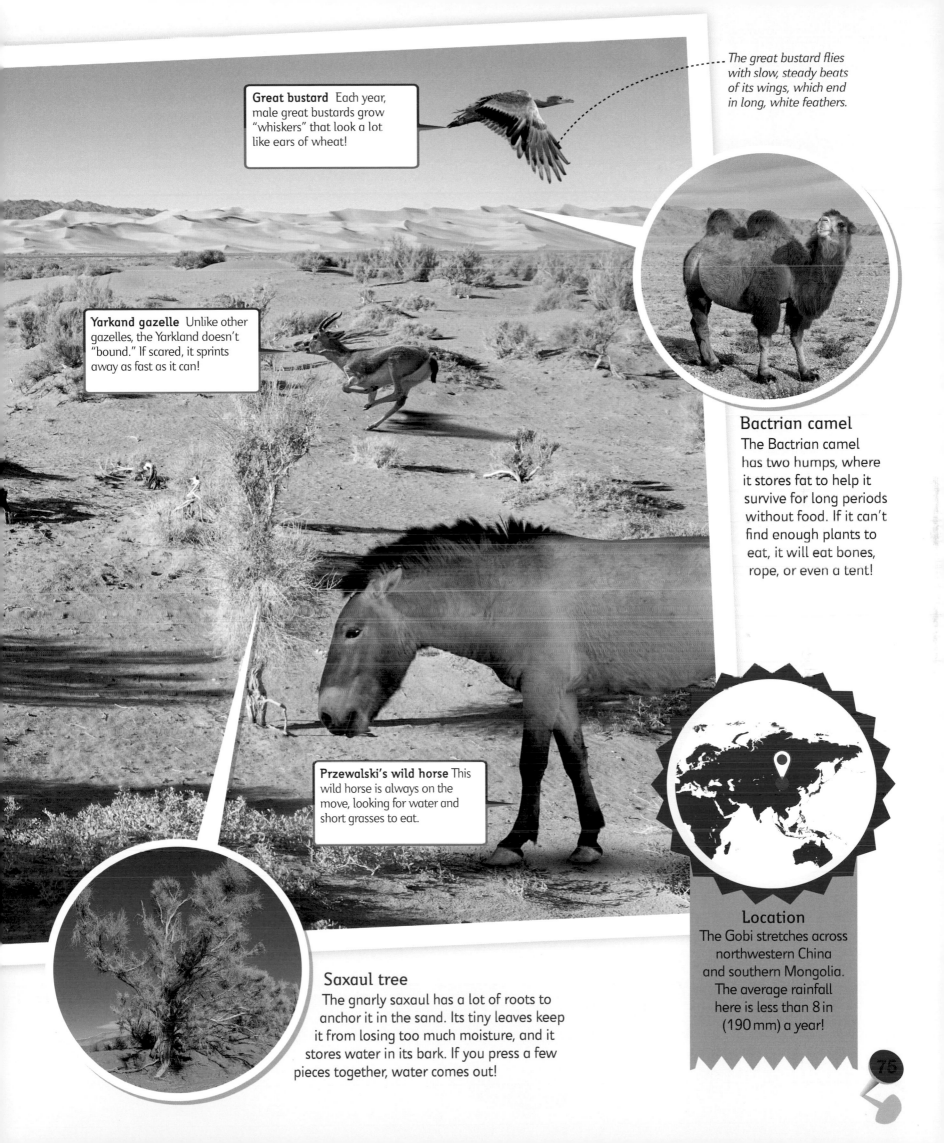

The great bustard flies with slow, steady beats of its wings, which end in long, white feathers.

Great bustard Each year, male great bustards grow "whiskers" that look a lot like ears of wheat!

Yarkand gazelle Unlike other gazelles, the Yarkland doesn't "bound." If scared, it sprints away as fast as it can!

Bactrian camel
The Bactrian camel has two humps, where it stores fat to help it survive for long periods without food. If it can't find enough plants to eat, it will eat bones, rope, or even a tent!

Przewalski's wild horse This wild horse is always on the move, looking for water and short grasses to eat.

Location
The Gobi stretches across northwestern China and southern Mongolia. The average rainfall here is less than 8 in (190 mm) a year!

Saxaul tree
The gnarly saxaul has a lot of roots to anchor it in the sand. Its tiny leaves keep it from losing too much moisture, and it stores water in its bark. If you press a few pieces together, water comes out!

75

Australasia

Australia, New Zealand, Papua New Guinea, and thousands of small islands make up the Australasia region. From deserts, mountains, and rain forests to beaches and coral reefs, the habitats here are home to many animals only found in this part of the world.

Australian coast
The western Australian coast is home to hundreds of fish, mammals, and bird species. Australian pelicans often land here to enjoy the sand and sun after long fishing trips.

PHILIPPINE SEA

Northern Mariana Islands
(UNITED STATES)

Guam
(UNITED STATES)

MICRONESIA

PALAU

PAPUA NEW GUINEA

ARAFURA SEA

TIMOR SEA

Coral Sea Islands
(AUSTRALIA)

CORAL SEA

Christmas Island
(AUSTRALIA)

Ashmore and Cartier Islands
(AUSTRALIA)

Cocos (Keeling) Islands
(AUSTRALIA)

INDIAN OCEAN

Northern Territory

Queensland

AUSTRALIA

Western Australia

South Australia

New South Wales

Victoria

Tasmania

N W E S

Macquarie Island
(AUSTRALIA)

Australian outback
The hot, dry center of Australia is known as the outback, or the "bush." Because it is mostly desert, very few people live here, but some amazing animals have found ways to survive the tough desert conditions.

Snares Islands
This New Zealand island group, north of the Auckland Islands, is protected from humans so native animal species can thrive. One is the Snares penguin, which nests only on these islands—on the ground, under trees and shrubs.

New Guinea forests

Forests cover two-thirds of the island of Papua New Guinea. Around 760 bird species and 25,000 plant species live here, as does the Goodfellow's tree kangaroo, which climbs trees to eat leaves.

Coral reefs

Coral reefs, like this one in French Polynesia, make up about one percent of the ocean floor—but they are home to almost a quarter of all ocean species. Lots of fish, such as these gold-lined sea breams, gather in the reefs to eat.

Wake Island
(UNITED STATES)

MARSHALL ISLANDS

NAURU

Kingman Reef
(UNITED STATES)

Baker and Howland Islands
(UNITED STATES)

Palmyra Atoll
(UNITED STATES)

Jarvis Island
(UNITED STATES)

KIRIBATI

SOLOMON ISLANDS

TUVALU

Wallis and Futuna
(FRANCE)

SAMOA

American Samoa
(UNITED STATES)

VANUATU

FIJI

Niue
(NEW ZEALAND)

TONGA

New Caledonia
(FRANCE)

Cook Islands
(NEW ZEALAND)

Norfolk Island
(AUSTRALIA)

Kermadec Islands
(NEW ZEALAND)

French Polynesia
(FRANCE)

Lord Howe Island
(AUSTRALIA)

PACIFIC OCEAN

NEW ZEALAND

TASMAN SEA

Chatham Islands
(NEW ZEALAND)

Bounty Islands
(NEW ZEALAND)

Auckland Islands
(NEW ZEALAND)

Antipodes Islands
(NEW ZEALAND)

Campbell Islands
(NEW ZEALAND)

Pitcairn, Henderson, Ducie, and Oeno Islands
(UNITED KINGDOM)

HABITAT KEY

- Tropical forests
- Deciduous forests
- Tropical grasslands
- Scrublands
- Temperate grasslands
- Desert
- Mountains
- Mangroves

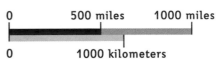

SCALE

0   500 miles   1000 miles

0   1000 kilometers

Australia

Australia is the world's largest island. Most of it is made of hot, dry desert called "the outback." In the hottest months, some of Australia's lakes may dry up completely. However, there are rain forests here, too, and many of the animals that live in Australia are found nowhere else.

Location

Australia lies south of the equator, between the Pacific and Indian oceans. Summer here is from December to February.

HABITAT KEY

- Temperate grasslands
- Tropical forests
- Scrublands
- Mountains
- Tropical grasslands
- Hot desert

This lizard defends itself by opening its frill, standing on its hind legs, and hissing.

Frilled lizard

The kookaburra is the largest kingfisher. Its call sounds like a laugh.

Blue-winged kookaburra

Victoria

Fitzroy

INDIAN OCEAN

De Grey

Fortescue

Ashburton

Gascoyne

This desert lizard is covered in protective thorny scales.

Thorny devil

AUSTRALIA

These huge caterpillars eat witchetty bush roots—and Australian Aboriginals, the first people to live here, eat them!

Witchetty grubs

Common off the Australian coast, the world's largest predatory fish has 300 teeth.

Great white shark

This mouse-sized marsupial doesn't eat honey—just nectar and pollen.

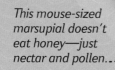

Honey possum

Emu

Australia's largest bird is 5–6½ ft (1.5–2 m) tall and can weigh up to 132 lb (60 kg). Its call can be heard up to 1 mile (2 km) away!

N
W   E
S

Red kangaroo

Kangaroos are marsupials, which are a type of animal that carry their young in a pouch on their body. Red kangaroos are only found in Australia. They move by hopping around on their powerful back legs.

A baby kangaroo, called a joey, rides in its mother's pouch.

Earth's largest reptile is also found in India and Southeast Asia.

Saltwater crocodile

Redbacks are one of the most venomous of Australia's 10,000 spider species.

Redback spider

Mitchell

Flinders

GREAT BARRIER REEF

The short-beaked echidna's sharp spines repel predators.

Short-beaked echidna

Also called the spiny anteater, this strange-looking mammal lays eggs. It uses its long, sticky tongue to eat grubs, termites, and ants.

This dangerous snake is responsible for the most deaths by snakebite in Australia. Watch out!

Eastern brown snake

Sugar glider

A webbed membrane allows this tiny mammal to glide more than 151 ft (46 m) between trees.

This intelligent wild dog rarely barks, but it loves to howl.

This plant-eating burrower is a marsupial, but its pouch points backward. Also, its poop is cube shaped!

Dingo

Common wombat

Darling

BLUE MOUNTAINS

Platypus

Murray

Canberra

This egg-laying mammal has webbed feet and a ducklike bill.

TASMAN SEA

GREAT
AUSTRALIAN
BIGHT

This animal is the size of a small dog. It's called a devil because it is so aggressive.

Tasmanian devil

Koala

Often mistakenly called bears, koalas are marsupials. Once big enough to leave the pouch, baby koalas ride on the parents' backs. Koalas mostly eat eucalyptus (gum tree) leaves, such as those found in southeastern Australia.

79

New Zealand

New Zealand is made up of two main islands—North and South Island—and many smaller ones. Lots of birds live here, some of which cannot fly. Unfortunately, many were killed by cats, rats, and other predators brought by European settlers. Now, rare birds such as the kakapo are protected.

Auckland tree weta

Wetas are much larger cousins of crickets. A tree weta's body is about 1½in (4cm) long, but a giant weta can be 4in (10cm)— longer than your hand!

Auckland tree wetas can raise their spiny back legs for defense.

These huge trees only grow on the North Island. Birds eat the seeds from the cones they produce.

Kauri

This bus-sized whale often raises its tail like a sail, letting the wind push it along the surface of the ocean.

Southern right whale

New Zealand's national symbol, the kiwi is a bird that cannot fly. It lives mostly in burrows and only comes out at night.

North Island brown kiwi

This rare frog lives mostly on tiny Stephens Island, where it is safe from tuataras and rats.

Hamilton's frog

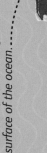

Bats are New Zealand's only native mammals. This one spends more time on the ground than in the air.

New Zealand lesser short-tailed bat

This enormous snail grows to 3½in (9cm) across and loves to eat earthworms.

New Zealand land snail

North Island

BAY OF PLENTY

Hawke Bay

Lake Taupo

Waikato

TASMAN SEA

Wellington

N E S W

Location

Located in the southwestern Pacific Ocean, New Zealand's closest neighbor is Australia, 932 miles (1,500km) to the northwest.

SCALE

0   250 miles

0   250 kilometers

Its large eyes help the nocturnal morepork to see at night.

Morepork

This small, dark owl got its name because its call sounds like "more pork"! It sleeps in forests during the day. At night it hunts insects, such as the weta.

Kea

Scientists think this cat-sized parrot is as smart as a four-year-old child. It lives on the South Island and makes a laughlike squeal.

Tuatara

This reptile's closest relatives were around at the time of the dinosaurs. Tuataras like cool weather and can live for up to 100 years!

PACIFIC OCEAN

Also called the kereru, this blue-green bird eats mostly fruit. It has a red bill, eyes, and feet.

New Zealand pigeon

The yellow-eyed penguin lays its eggs in forests, and hunts for food up to 15 miles (24km) away.

Yellow-eyed penguin

This sea lion rests on southern beaches and offshore islands when it isn't hunting squid.

New Zealand sea lion

South Island

Lake Tekapo

Lake Pukaki

Lake Ohau

SOUTHERN ALPS

Lake Hawea

Lake Wanaka

Clutha

Northern koura

Hector's dolphin

Found only in New Zealand, this crayfish buries itself in mud to survive droughts.

Highly endangered, this social little dolphin only grows up to 4½ft (1.4m) long.

Blue damselfly

Lake Te Anau

The blue damselfly can turn itself darker to get more warmth from the sun.

So rare they are almost extinct, these large, flightless parrots live only in New Zealand.

Kakapo

Stewart Island

TASMAN SEA

HABITAT KEY

Temperate grasslands

Deciduous forests

Mountains

Great Barrier Reef

The world's largest chain of coral reefs, the Great Barrier Reef lies just off Australia's northeastern coast. It's so big that it can be seen from space, and it is home to more than 1,500 types of fish.

Regal tang Also called surgeonfish, tangs have a scalpel-like spine at the base of their tail on both sides.

Giant barrel sponge The barrel sponge is an animal that grows up to 6 ft (1.8 m) across—and it has no brain!

Sea slug Sea slugs eat corals, sea anemones, sponges, and fish eggs. Their bright colors warn predators away.

Dugongs can live for 70 years or more in the wild.

Dugong

This slow-moving mammal eats nothing but plants. It pulls seagrass out by the roots with its flexible upper lip. Dugongs are also called "sea cows," because they graze like cows.

Coral

Living corals are made up of tiny animals called coral polyps that catch bits of food with their tentacles. The polyps make hard cases from minerals to protect themselves, and these build up over many years into a reef.

Blue starfish Tiny suckers, called tube feet, cover the underside of starfish and let them crawl over the reef.

The reef has many different types of coral. In addition to hard corals, which build the reef, there are also soft corals.

Starfish can regrow a damaged or lost arm. Some can even grow a whole new starfish from just part of an arm.

Blubber jellyfish Each of this creature's eight stumpy arms has several mouths that move food to the animal's stomach.

Blacktip reef shark This medium-sized shark loves the shallows. It can swim in water just 12 in (30 cm) deep.

Potato cod The potato cod hunts fish, crabs, and crayfish. It's so curious that it can annoy divers.

The peacock mantis shrimp has the fastest punch in the animal world.

Peacock mantis shrimp

Only 1–7 in (3–18 cm) long, this shrimp is deadly. Its clublike arms can punch hard enough to break the shells of crabs—and even aquarium glass!

Green sea turtle Green sea turtles are black when they hatch. They change color over the next 25 to 50 years.

Olive sea snake This snake breathes air, and it has a large lung that lets it swim for hours between breaths.

Orange clown fish Clown fish have coats of slime that let them live in sea anemones without being stung.

Location

The Great Barrier Reef runs for 1,429 miles (2,300 km) off the coast of the state of Queensland, Australia.

Giant clam

This clam is so big, it can no longer move. It lives attached to the reef, where it sucks in plankton to eat with a tubelike organ called a siphon.

Most sea creatures avoid sea anemones because they sting, but clown fish live among their tentacles for protection. In return, they bring the anemones food.

Antarctica

The world's coldest continent, Antarctica is also its most remote, meaning it is far from any other land mass. Ice more than 1 mile (1.6 km) thick covers most of it, and temperatures go down to -129°F (-89.2°C), too extreme for many animals. Since it doesn't rain here, Antarctica is considered a desert.

Location

Antarctica is found at the bottom of the Earth. It is home to the Earth's most southerly point, the South Pole.

HABITAT KEY

 Snow and ice

Mountains

Southern elephant seal

The southern elephant seal is Earth's largest seal. Males can grow up to 20 ft (6 m) long and weigh 8,501 lb (3,856 kg), but females are much smaller. An inflatable, trunklike nose allows males to make loud roaring calls.

Wandering albatross

With the longest wingspan of any bird—11½ ft (3.5 m) —the wandering albatross can glide for hours at a time.

Blackfin icefish

This fish's blood is white because it has no red blood cells. This makes it easier for blood to move around the body in icy water.

ANTARCTIC PENINSULA

WEDDELL SEA

Weddell seals can stay underwater for up to 82 minutes while they hunt for icefish.

Weddell seal

FILCHNER ICE SHELF

RONNE ICE SHELF

Chinstrap penguin

These penguins look as if they have a strap around their chin. They are often found on icebergs in the sea around Antarctica.

Like most Antarctic fish, the toothfish has chemicals in its blood that prevent it from freezing.

Patagonian toothfish

So... Po...

West Antarctica

This small whale catches krill by using comblike structures in its mouth called baleen.

Antarctic minke whale

TO SOUTH AMERICA

ICE

SCALE

0	250 miles
0	250 kilometers

TO NEW ZEALAND

Limit of winter pack ice

Limit of summer pack ice

SOUTHERN OCEAN

Even though it has enormous jaws and eats other animals, this seal's main food is tiny krill.

Leopard seal

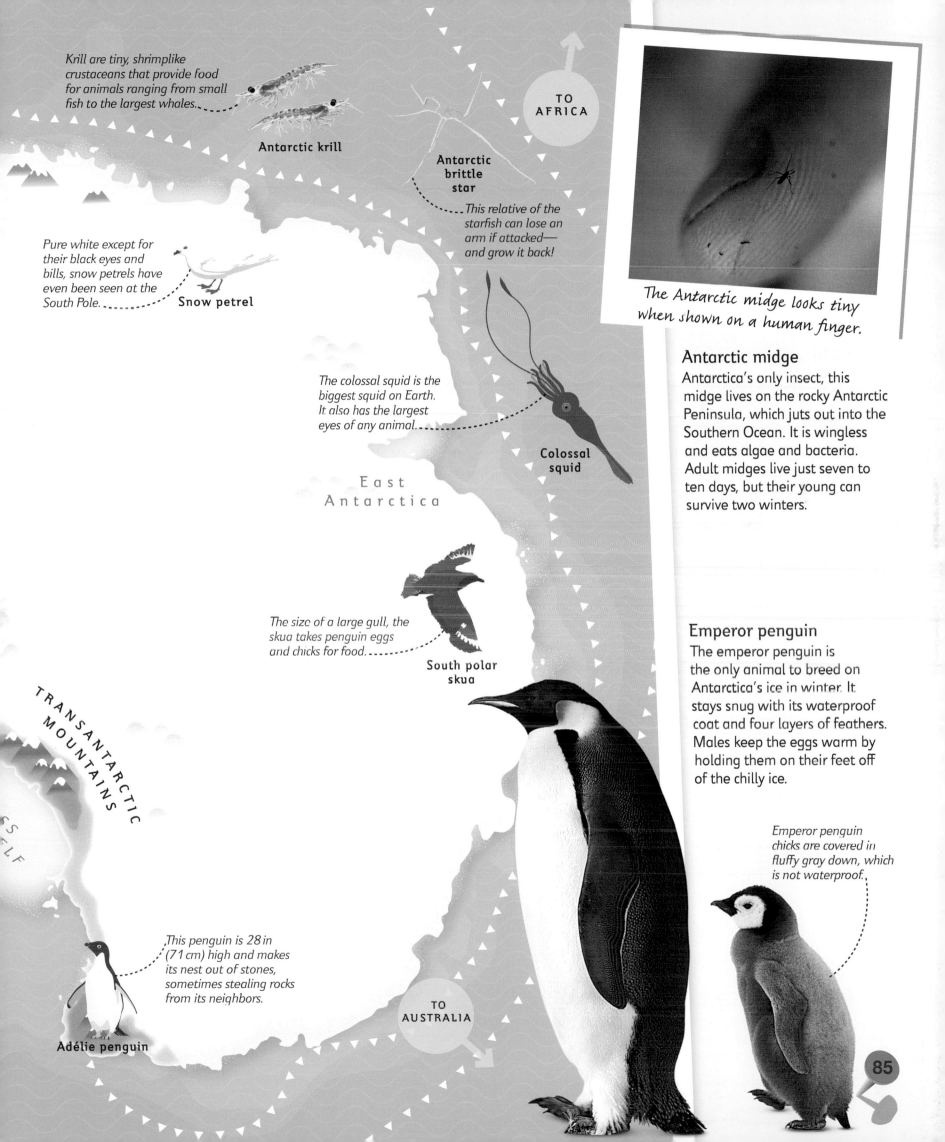

Krill are tiny, shrimplike crustaceans that provide food for animals ranging from small fish to the largest whales.

Antarctic krill

TO AFRICA

Antarctic brittle star

This relative of the starfish can lose an arm if attacked—and grow it back!

Pure white except for their black eyes and bills, snow petrels have even been seen at the South Pole.

Snow petrel

The colossal squid is the biggest squid on Earth. It also has the largest eyes of any animal.

Colossal squid

E a s t
A n t a r c t i c a

The size of a large gull, the skua takes penguin eggs and chicks for food.

South polar skua

T R A N S A N T A R C T I C
M O U N T A I N S

S S
E L F

This penguin is 28 in (71 cm) high and makes its nest out of stones, sometimes stealing rocks from its neighbors.

Adélie penguin

TO AUSTRALIA

The Antarctic midge looks tiny when shown on a human finger.

Antarctic midge

Antarctica's only insect, this midge lives on the rocky Antarctic Peninsula, which juts out into the Southern Ocean. It is wingless and eats algae and bacteria. Adult midges live just seven to ten days, but their young can survive two winters.

Emperor penguin

The emperor penguin is the only animal to breed on Antarctica's ice in winter. It stays snug with its waterproof coat and four layers of feathers. Males keep the eggs warm by holding them on their feet off of the chilly ice.

Emperor penguin chicks are covered in fluffy gray down, which is not waterproof.

The Arctic

The Arctic is the Earth's northernmost region. Animals here must survive freezing temperatures. Ice and snow cover the area in winter, and the water of the Arctic Ocean freezes over. In summer, much of the ice melts, revealing a treeless habitat on the surrounding land called tundra.

Polar bear

The polar bear actually has black skin, but it is covered by thick fur to keep the bear warm. A strong swimmer, the polar bear hunts seals, which it can smell from 1 mile (1.6 km) away.

A polar bear's white fur helps it blend in with its habitat.

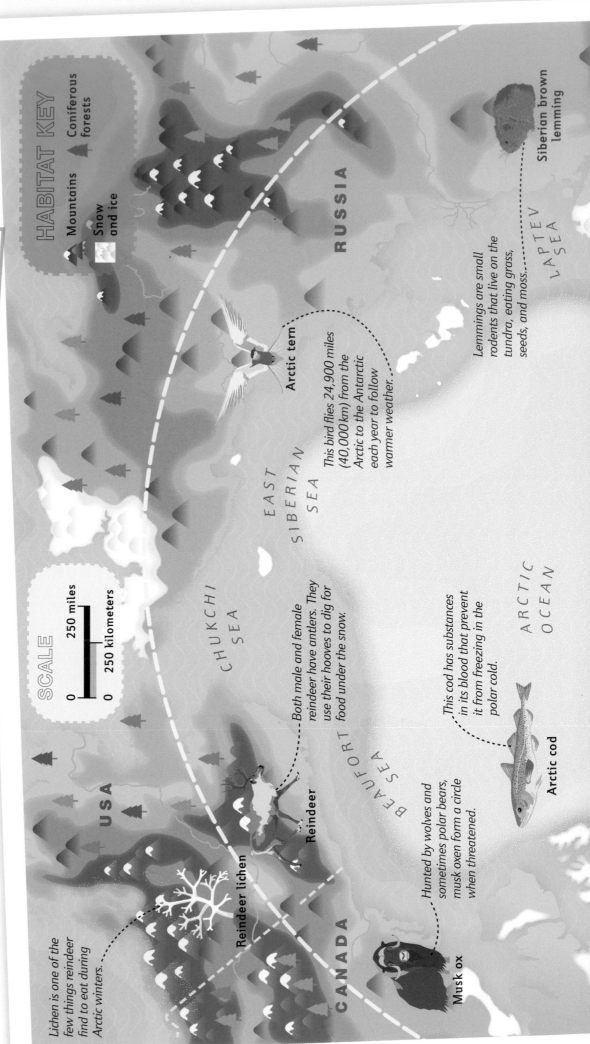

HABITAT KEY

- ▲ Mountains
- ▲ Coniferous forests
- Snow and ice

RUSSIA

Siberian brown lemming

Lemmings are small rodents that live on the tundra, eating grass, seeds, and moss.

LAPTEV SEA

Arctic tern

This bird flies 24,900 miles (40,000 km) from the Arctic to the Antarctic each year to follow warmer weather.

EAST SIBERIAN SEA

CHUKCHI SEA

SCALE

```
0        250 miles
0        250 kilometers
```

Both male and female reindeer have antlers. They use their hooves to dig for food under the snow.

Reindeer

BEAUFORT SEA

ARCTIC OCEAN

Arctic cod

This cod has substances in its blood that prevent it from freezing in the polar cold.

Reindeer lichen

USA

Hunted by wolves and sometimes polar bears, musk oxen form a circle when threatened.

CANADA

Musk ox

Lichen is one of the few things reindeer find to eat during Arctic winters.

Snowy owl

KARA SEA

BARENTS SEA

GREENLAND SEA

NORWAY

FINLAND

SWEDEN

Born gray, beluga whales don't turn white until they are as old as eight years.

Beluga

This whale's spiral tusk is actually a tooth that grows up to 10 ft (3 m) long.

Narwhal

North Pole

Greenland shark

A very slow swimmer, this shark cruises deep in the ocean, feeding on carrion (dead animals).

Walrus

A thick layer of blubber (fat) keeps walruses warm when they hunt for food in icy waters.

Lemmings are one of the snowy owl's main sources of food. It can eat five lemmings in a day.

Its pure-white coat makes this hare almost invisible in the snow.

Arctic hare

Arctic fox

In winter, this fox turns white to help it hide in the snow as it hunts for Arctic hares.

GREENLAND (DENMARK)

Location
The Arctic includes the extreme northern parts of Europe, Asia, and North America. Winters get as cold as -90°F (-68°C).

Harp seal
These seals are named for the pattern on their backs, which looks like the musical instrument. Harp seals are born white, but turn dark after three weeks.

Arctic fox
In summer, the Arctic fox sheds its white coat, turning gray-brown so it blends in with its surroundings.

An adult harp seal watches its white-furred cub.

87

HABITAT KEY

Coral reef

The chinook hatches in freshwater, then swims to the ocean, but each adult fish returns to the place where it hatched to breed.

Chinook salmon

The cuttlefish is related to squids and octopuses.

Common cuttlefish

The cuttlefish changes color to blend in with its surroundings and to communicate with other cuttlefish. It has three hearts, two of which pump blood to its gills. The third pumps blood around its body.

Sardines grow up to 12 in (30 cm) long and swim in enormous schools with lots of other sardines so they aren't all eaten at once.

Sardines

The world's largest ray, the giant manta grows up to 23 ft (7 m) across and weighs up to 2.2 tons (2 tonnes).

Giant manta ray

As it grows, the lobster sheds its skin—a process called molting. By the time it becomes an adult, a lobster has increased in size 100,000 times!

American lobster

Killer whale

Also known as an orca, this is the largest dolphin species. It has teeth up to 4 in (10 cm) long.

Blue mussels

The blue mussel is one of the toughest shellfish around. It can survive freezing as well as very warm ocean water.

Yellowfin tuna

Just one yellowfin tuna can weigh up to 882 lb (400 kg), although 388 lb (176 kg) is more common.

Great hammerhead

The great hammerhead's favorite food is the stingray. It holds rays down using one side of its "hammer" to avoid getting stung while it feeds.

The sea horse can move its eyes individually, so it can watch for predators or prey from many directions at once.

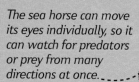

Spiny sea horse

PACIFIC OCEAN

The anglerfish uses the glowing lure on its head to tempt passing prey close enough to eat.

Deep sea anglerfish

ATLANTIC OCEAN

Blue whale

The blue whale is roughly the size of a jumbo jet. It weighs two times more than the biggest known dinosaur.

Oceans and seas

Water covers a huge 70 percent of the Earth's surface. Thousands of species live in or near oceans and seas, from tiny plankton to the largest creature on our planet—the blue whale.

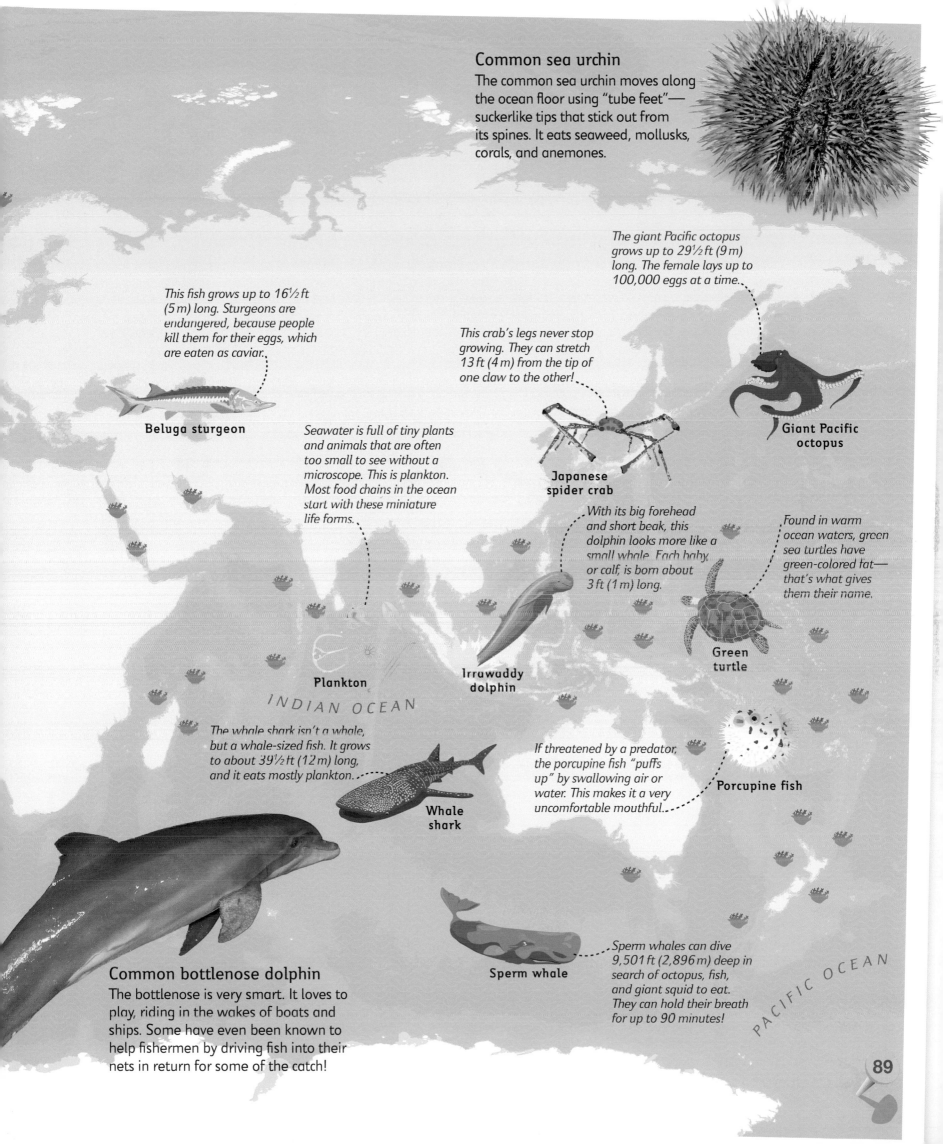

Common sea urchin

The common sea urchin moves along the ocean floor using "tube feet"—suckerlike tips that stick out from its spines. It eats seaweed, mollusks, corals, and anemones.

The giant Pacific octopus grows up to 29½ ft (9 m) long. The female lays up to 100,000 eggs at a time.

This fish grows up to 16½ ft (5 m) long. Sturgeons are endangered, because people kill them for their eggs, which are eaten as caviar.

This crab's legs never stop growing. They can stretch 13 ft (4 m) from the tip of one claw to the other!

Beluga sturgeon

Seawater is full of tiny plants and animals that are often too small to see without a microscope. This is plankton. Most food chains in the ocean start with these miniature life forms.

Japanese spider crab

Giant Pacific octopus

With its big forehead and short beak, this dolphin looks more like a small whale. Each baby, or calf, is born about 3 ft (1 m) long.

Found in warm ocean waters, green sea turtles have green-colored fat—that's what gives them their name.

Plankton

INDIAN OCEAN

Irrawaddy dolphin

Green turtle

The whale shark isn't a whale, but a whale-sized fish. It grows to about 39½ ft (12 m) long, and it eats mostly plankton.

If threatened by a predator, the porcupine fish "puffs up" by swallowing air or water. This makes it a very uncomfortable mouthful.

Porcupine fish

Whale shark

Sperm whale

Sperm whales can dive 9,501 ft (2,896 m) deep in search of octopus, fish, and giant squid to eat. They can hold their breath for up to 90 minutes!

Common bottlenose dolphin

The bottlenose is very smart. It loves to play, riding in the wakes of boats and ships. Some have even been known to help fishermen by driving fish into their nets in return for some of the catch!

PACIFIC OCEAN

ATLAS PICTURE QUIZ

This area in northern Africa is the largest hot desert in the world.

1

2

This area of scrubland shares its name with the sea it borders.

This high prairie stretches across parts of Canada and the United States.

3

10

This famous mountain range in Europe includes lakes, glaciers, meadows, and forests.

NAME THE HABITAT

Here are some of the habitats and islands that appear in this atlas. Can you name them? Look at the clues to help you. The answers are on page 91.

4

This country is made of two main islands and lots of other, smaller ones.

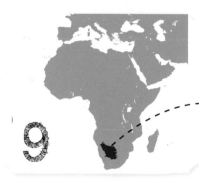

This desert in southern Africa gets enough rain for grass and other plants to grow.

9

This South American rain forest is home to 2.5 million different species of insects.

5

The rain forests of this area are some of the oldest on Earth.

8

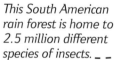

7

6

These volcanic islands are home to many unique animals named after the area.

This continent, found at the bottom of the Earth, is the world's coldest.

All of the answers to these questions appear somewhere in this book. You can check if you are correct at the bottom of this page.

3. How many ants can an aardvark eat a night?

2. What sea creature has the largest eyes of any animal?

1. What is the smallest of the "big cats"?

4. What color, other than blue, can the Mediterranean tree frog be?

5. For how long does a seven-spot ladybug live?

6. In what mountain range would you find the spectacled bear?

7. How long do the Iberian ibex's horns grow?

11. In what area would you find a mandrill?

10. What is the largest tortoise in Africa?

9. Where does the Gila monster live?

8. What animal has cube-shaped poop?

12. What lizard is also called the racerunner?

13. What bird has two tail feathers twice the length of its body?

14. What whale has a tusk that can grow to 10ft (3m) long?

15. On what island does the ring-tailed lemur live?

19. What butterfly migrates from northern North America to Mexico?

18. What penguin lays its eggs in forests?

17. What is the heaviest spider in the world?

16. What is the heaviest flying bird on Earth?

20. What bat drinks other animals' blood?

21. How long can the Indian tiger's fangs grow?

22. What frog uses its feet to parachute from tree to tree?

23. What beetle with antlerlike jaws is this?

Answers: Page 90 Name the habitat: 1. Sahara desert (pages 36–37), 2. Mediterranean scrubland (pages 56–57), 3. Great Plains (page 12), 4. New Zealand (pages 80–81), 5. Amazon rain forest (pages 22–23), 6. Antarctica (pages 84–85), 7. Southeast Asia (pages 72–73), 8. The Galapagos (pages 29), 9. Kalahari (page 42), 10. The Alps (page 54).
Page 91 Guess the icon: 1. Clouded leopard (page 68), 2. Colossal squid (page 85), 3. 50,000 (page 42), 4. Green (page 51), 5. The Andes (page 56), 6. One year (page 24), 7. 29½in or 75 cm (page 56),
8. Common wombat (page 79), 9. American western deserts (page 14), 10. African spurred tortoise (page 31), 11. Congo Basin (page 38), 12. Giant ameiva (page 37), 13. Resplendent quetzal (page 16),
14. Narwhal (page 87), 15. Madagascar (page 43), 16. Great bustard (page 55), 17. Goliath birdeater (page 23), 18. Yellow-eyed penguin (page 81), 19. Monarch butterfly (page 11), 20. Vampire bat (page 17),
21. 4in or 10cm (page 71), 22. Wallace's flying frog (page 72), 23. Stag beetle (page 52).

Glossary

amphibians
Cold-blooded animals that live both on land and in water, such as frogs and newts

birds
Warm-blooded animals that are covered in feathers and have a bill, many of which can fly, such as eagles

climate
Normal weather pattern during the year in any part of the world

coniferous tree
Type of tree with cones and needlelike leaves that keeps its leaves all year round

continents
Seven large areas of land that the world is divided into: Africa, Antarctica, Asia, Australasia, Europe, North America, and South America

coral reefs
Rocklike structures formed by coral animals in the shallow waters along coasts

deciduous tree
Type of tree that loses its leaves in the fall or the dry season

desert
Dry region that gets very little rainfall in a year. Deserts can be hot or cold

endangered
Word used to describe a species of plant or animal with only a few living members left

equator
Imaginary line around the middle of the Earth

extinct
Word used to describe a plant or animal species that has no living members

fish
Cold-blooded animals that live in water and have gills and fins, such as salmon

habitat
Environment in which an animal or plant lives

hibernation
Sleeplike state some animals enter in winter

invertebrates
Cold-blooded animals without a backbone, such as insects, spiders, or squids

island
Piece of land that has water all around it

mammals
Warm-blooded animals that have hair and feed their young with milk, such as mice

mangroves
Trees that live in salty water and have long, stiltlike roots

marsupial
Type of mammal that keeps its young in a pouch

migration
Movement of a large number of animals from one area to another. Animals migrate to follow warmer weather and to find food

mountain
Area of land that rises up much higher than the land around it to form a peak

national park
Area of countryside that has been preserved in its natural state by the government of a country to protect the wildlife there and for people to enjoy

native
Word used to describe an animal that comes from a particular area or country

nocturnal
Word used to describe animals that are awake during the night

ocean
Very large sea. There are five oceans: the Pacific, Atlantic, Indian, Arctic, and Southern

plain
Area of flat land with few trees, often covered with grass

plateau
Large area of high, flat land

polar regions
Areas within the polar circles. Polar regions are covered in snow and ice for most of the year and are extremely cold

predator
Animal that hunts other living animals for food

prey
Animal that is hunted for food

rain forests
Dense forests with very high rainfall. Most are near the equator and are also very hot

reptiles
Cold-blooded animals covered in dry, scaly skin such as snakes, tortoises, and crocodiles

scrubland
Area of land covered in different types of grass, and small trees and bushes

species
Particular group of animals or plants that share similar features

taiga
Area of cold, coniferous forest found near the Arctic Circle

temperate grassland
Large areas of grass found in regions with hot and cold seasons, such as prairie, steppe, and pampas

temperate regions
Areas with hot and cold seasons found between tropical and polar regions

tropical grassland
Large areas of grass found in areas that are hot all year round, such as savanna and cerrado

tropical regions
Areas that are hot all year round, found near the equator between the Tropic of Cancer and the Tropic of Capricorn

tundra
Cold, treeless plains found near the Arctic Circle

wetlands
Land with wet, spongy soil, such as a marsh or swamp

Index

Credits

Dorling Kindersley would like to thank Dr. Don E. Wilson, Curator Emeritus, Department of Vertebrate Zoology, National Museum of Natural History, Smithsonian, for his expert consultation.

The publisher would also like to thank the following people for their help in preparing this book: Kealy Gordon and Ellen Nanney at the Smithsonian; Helen Peters for the index; Polly Goodman for proofreading; Joylon Goddard and Katy Lennon for additional editing; and Jagtar Singh and Sachin Singh for additional design.

Picture Credits:
The publisher would also like to thank the following for their kind permission to reproduce their photographs:

(Key: a-above; b-below/bottom; c-center; f-far; l-left; r-right; t-top)

8 Alamy Stock Photo: John Hyde / Design Pics Inc (c). **iStockphoto.com:** ericfoltz (bl); Pawel Gaul (cl). **9 iStockphoto.com:** John_Wijsman (tr); OGphoto (cr). **11 Alamy Stock Photo:** Danny Green / Nature Picture Library (tl); Vl_K (tr). **Dorling Kindersley:** Jerry Young (br). **12 123RF.com:** wrangel (br). **Corbis:** Ocean (cl). **13 123RF.com:** Marie-Ann Daloia (cr). **Dorling Kindersley:** Jerry Young (tl). **14 Alamy Stock Photo:** Wayne Lynch / All Canada Photos (tc). **SuperStock:** Cyril Ruoso / Minden Pictures (cl). **16 Fotolia:** Eric Isselee (cl). **17 Photolibrary:** Photodisc / Tom Brakefield (tr). **18 Alamy Stock Photo:** WaterFrame_eda (cl). **Dorling Kindersley:** Jerry Young (cr). **Dreamstime.com:** Brian Lasenby (cb). **Getty Images:** Joe McDonald / Corbis Documentary (bl). **18-19 Getty Images:** Tim Graham / Getty Images News. **19 Alamy Stock Photo:** George Grall / National Geographic Creative (bl). **iStockphoto.com:** FernandoAH (tl); madcorona (crb); hakoar (tr); ygluzberg (b). **20 Alamy Stock Photo:** Denis-Huot Michel / hemis.fr / Hemis (bl). **iStockphoto.com:** Marcelo Horn (cl). 21 **123RF.com:** belikova (b). **Alamy Stock Photo:** blickwinkel / Wothe (cr). **iStockphoto.com:** Magaiza (tr). **22 iStockphoto.com:** Leonardo Prest Mercon Ro / LeoMercon (cl). **23 123RF.com:** Anan Kaewkhammul (br). **Alamy Stock Photo:** Amazon-Images (cra). **24 SuperStock:** Albert Lleal / Minden Pictures (tc). **25 Dorling Kindersley:** Blackpool Zoo (br). **iStockphoto.com:** webguzs (bl). **26 SuperStock:** Juniors (cl). **27 Alamy Stock Photo:** Johner Images (tr). **Dorling Kindersley:** Gary Ombler (br). **28 123RF.com:** Francisco de Casa Gonzalez (br); Ondřej Prosický (tr). **Alamy Stock Photo:** James Brunker (bl). **29 123RF.com:** mark52 (bl). **Alamy Stock Photo:** Reinhard Dirscherl (cr). **30 Dorling Kindersley:** Greg Dean / Yvonne Dean (cl). **31 naturepl.com:** Luiz Claudio Marigo (br). **SuperStock:** Minden Pictures (cra). **32 123RF.com:** Martin Otero (cl). **Dorling Kindersley:** Hanne Eriksen / Jens Eriksen (fcrb); Prof. Marcio Motta (cb). **Dreamstime.com:** Jeremy Richards (bl). **33 123RF.com:** Martin Schneiter (c). **Dorling Kindersley:** E. J. Peiker (tr). **Dreamstime.com:** Musat Christian (cr). **SuperStock:** Glenn Bartley / All Canada Photos (bl, tl). **34 Alamy Stock Photo:** Michele Burgess (bc); Lars Johansson (cl).

35 Alamy Stock Photo: Ange (br); Aivar Mikko (tc). **iStockphoto.com:** helovi (cra). **36 Dorling Kindersley:** Jerry Young (br). **38 Dorling Kindersley:** Liberty's Owl, Raptor and Reptile Centre, Hampshire, UK (bl). **39 123RF.com:** Andrey Gudkov (cr); Jatesada Natayo (tr). **41 123RF.com:** pytyczech (bc). **Alamy Stock Photo:** Andrew Mackay (r). **42 Dorling Kindersley:** Wildlife Heritage Foundation, Kent, UK (bl). **Dreamstime.com:** Artushfoto (ftr). **SuperStock:** Alexander Koenders / NiS / Minden Pictures (tr). **43 Alamy Stock Photo:** Travel Africa (cl); Eric Nathan (br). **Dreamstime.com:** Faunuslsd (bl). **44 Depositphotos Inc:** Meoita (cb). **Dorling Kindersley:** Blackpool Zoo, Lancashire, UK (crb). **Dreamstime.com:** Lauren Pretorius (bl). **SuperStock:** Biosphoto (cl); Roger de la Harpe / Africa (c). **45 Dorling Kindersley:** Suzanne Porter / Rough Guides (fcra). **Dreamstime.com:** Clickit (c); Ecophoto (tr); Rixie (cra); Mark De Scande (cr); Fabio Lamanna (bc). **46 Dreamstime.com:** Philip Bird (c). **iStockphoto.com:** nimu1956 (db). **47 Alamy Stock Photo:** Images & Stories (cr). **iStockphoto.com:** misterbike (tr); vencavolrab (bc). **49 Dorling Kindersley:** ZSL Whipsnade Zoo (tr). **Dreamstime.com:** Anagram1 (tl). **SuperStock:** Juniors (br). **50 123RF.com:** Piotr Krześlak (tc). **51 Dorling Kindersley:** Hoa Luc (br). **52 Dorling Kindersley:** British Wildlife Centre, Surrey, UK (bl). **53 123RF.com:** alucard21 (tr). **Dorling Kindersley:** Rollin Verlinde (bl). **54 Dorling Kindersley:** British Wildlife Centre, Surrey, UK (bl). **iStockphoto.com:** mauribo (br). **55 Dreamstime.com:** Mikelane45 (crb). **SuperStock:** Kurt Kracher / imagebro / imageBROKER (tr). **57 Dreamstime.com:** García Juan (tr); Rosemarie Kappler (tl). **58 Dorling Kindersley:** British Wildlife Centre, Surrey, UK (cr, c); Jerry Young (cl). **Dreamstime.com:** Valentino2 (bl). **58-59 Alamy Stock Photo:** Aleksander Bolbot. **59 123RF.com:** alein (tc); Alexey Sokolov (bl). **Dorling Kindersley:** Rollin Verlinde (ftr). **Fotolia:** Eric Isselee (cr). **60 Alamy Stock Photo:** Danita Delimont / Gavriel Jecan (cl); Ethiopia / Panther Media GmbH (bl). **iStockphoto.com:** Danielrao (tr). **61 Alamy Stock Photo:** Art Wolfe / Cultura RM (cr). **iStockphoto.com:** fotoVoyager (tr). **62 123RF.com:** Sergey Krasnoshchokov (cl). **Dorling Kindersley:** Blackpool Zoo (bl). **63 Dreamstime.com:** Silviu Matei (tl). **iStockphoto.com:** Gerdzhikov (br). **64 Dorling Kindersley:** Twan Leenders (tr). **65 Dreamstime.com:** Dmytro Pylypenko (tl). **66 Dreamstime.com:** Rudra Narayan Mitra (bc). **67 Dorling Kindersley:** Connor Daly (tr); Wildlife Heritage Foundation, Kent, UK (b). **68 Dreamstime.com:** Vasiliy Vishnevskiy (bl). **iStockphoto.com:** Biscut (cl). **69 Dorling Kindersley:** Jerry Young (br). **70 123RF.com:** Shlomo Polonsky (bl); wrangel (br). **Alamy Stock Photo:** blickwinkel / McPHOTO / MAS (tr). **71 123RF.com:** tonarinokeroro (cra). **SuperStock:** Biosphoto (br). **72 Dreamstime.com:** Phittavas (tl). **73 123RF.com:** aquafun (tr). **74-75 Alamy Stock Photo:** David Tipling Photo Library. **74 Dreamstime.com:** Evgovorov (bl). **naturepl.com:** Roland Seitre (cb). **SuperStock:** Biosphoto (cra, cr); Pete Oxford / Minden Pictures (crb); Stock Connection (cl). **75 Dreamstime.com:** Mikelane45 (tc);

Maxim Petrichuk (bl). **iStockphoto.com:** muha04 (cra). **SuperStock:** Biosphoto (ca). **76 Alamy Stock Photo:** David Foster (clb); Schöttger / mauritius images GmbH (cla); Frans Lanting Studio (bc). **77 Alamy Stock Photo:** WaterFrame_fba (tr). **SuperStock:** Roland Seitre / Minden Pictures (tl). **78 Alamy Stock Photo:** FLPA (br). **79 Fotolia:** Eric Isselee (br). **80 Getty Images:** Robin Bush / Oxford Scientific (bl). **81 123RF.com:** petervick167 (tl). **82 123RF.com:** Daniel Poloha (br). **Alamy Stock Photo:** Barry Brown / DanitaDelimont. com / Danita Delimont (cl). **iStockphoto.com:** Izanbar (cl). **iStockphoto.com:** LeventKonuk (bl). **SuperStock:** Fred Bavendam / Minden Pictures (tr); Ron Offermans / Buiten-beeld / Minden Pictures (cr). **82-83 Alamy Stock Photo:** Norbert Probst / imageBROKER. **83 123RF.com:** antos777 (cla). **Alamy Stock Photo:** Reinhard Dirscherl (br). **Dreamstime.com:** Carol Buchanan (bc); Apidech Ninkhlai (tc); Whitcomberd (tr). **SuperStock:** Fred Bavendam / Minden Pictures (db, ftl, tl); D. Parer & E. Parer-Cook / Minden Pictures (fbl). **84 Alamy Stock Photo:** David Osborn (bl). **85 Getty Images:** Bill Curtsinger / National Geographic (tr); David Tipling / Digital Vision (br). **86 123RF.com:** Ondřej Prosický (cla). **87 Alamy Stock Photo:** Arco / G. Lacz / Arco Images GmbH (tr). **Dorling Kindersley:** Jerry Young (br). **88 iStockphoto.com:** BulentBARIS (tc). **89 Dreamstime.com:** Igor Dolgov (tr).

All other images © Dorling Kindersley